GHOST STORIES *of* CHRISTMAS

Jo-Anne Christensen

Illustrations by Arlana Anderson-Hale

Lone Pine Publishing

The Publisher: Lone Pine Publishing

10145 – 81 Avenue
Edmonton, AB T6E 1W9
Canada

1901 Raymond Ave. Suite C
Renton, WA 98055
USA

Website: http://www.lonepinepublishing.com

National Library of Canada Cataloguing in Publication Data
Christensen, Jo-Anne.
  Ghost stories of Christmas

  ISBN 1-55105-334-9

  1. Ghosts. 2. Christmas. I. Title.
GR580.C56 2001   133.1   C2001-911346-3

Editorial Director: Nancy Foulds
Project Editor: Shelagh Kubish
Book Design, Layout & Production: Arlana Anderson-Hale
Cover Design: Arlana Anderson-Hale & Elliot Engley

We acknowledge the financial support of the Government of Canada through the Book Publishing Industry Development Program (BPIDP) for our publishing activities.

PC: P6

Dedication

For Dennis,
who has always had the best ideas,
including this one.

Contents

Acknowledgments

There are many good people who deserve to be acknowledged for their part in the creation of this book. Each has been tremendously helpful in his or her own way, and I wish to take this opportunity to express my gratitude.

The staff and management of Lone Pine Publishing have been wonderful, as always. In particular, I wish to thank Shelagh Kubish and Arlana Anderson-Hale for sharing their talents, and Shane Kennedy and Nancy Foulds for their continued support.

My sincere thanks goes out to W. Ritchie Benedict, of Calgary, Alberta—a researcher of seemingly limitless resourcefulness, who brought to my attention much of the information that is in the Introduction.

In my private life, I receive endless support from my dearest friend, Barbara Smith; my children, Steven, Grace, William and Natalie; and my husband, Dennis. Dennis is the source of many ideas in my writing life, and is owed credit for the entire concept of this particular book.

Finally, I wish to acknowledge as source material the correspondence and conversations I have shared with several generous people who wish to remain anonymous, as well as the following published works: *Ghost Stories of the Maritimes*, by Vernon Oickle (Lone Pine Publishing, 2001); the collected works of author Barbara Smith; *The Victoria Daily Colonist*, January 26, 1969; *FATE* magazine, April, 1969.

By sharing your stories, in whichever form, you have greatly enriched my experience as an author. You have provided the inspiration for the tales in this book and, for that, I thank you.

Introduction

"Bah," said Scrooge. "Humbug!"
   —Charles Dickens, *A Christmas Carol* (1843)

There is nothing quite so comfortable as an idea that has already proven successful. However, I was well into the writing of these stories before I realized that this book fell nicely into that category.

I started out thinking that "Christmas" and "ghosts" made for an odd sort of marriage. I was interested in the concept and was convinced that it would work, and I knew that there were plenty of stories about seasonal specters out there—but I wondered how others would feel about the idea.

Then I learned that I had been going about my business embarrassingly uninformed, and that since the early 1800s, the reading public has felt just fine about this particular combination of themes.

In a 1988 article for The Associated Press, Hugh Mulligan wrote, "The Christmas Ghost is older in tradition than the fir tree trimmed with lights," and "in Victorian times, a ghost for Christmas was as common as a goose."

Charles Dickens may be the only author who springs to mind when thinking of Christmas ghost stories—but, rest assured, he had plenty of prominent company and a publishing industry that was more than willing to provide the forum for their work.

From Victorian times through to the end of the Second World War, there were countless Christmas gift books and annuals devoted entirely to ghost stories. The presentation was upscale, and the list of contributors was often prestigious. Edgar Allen Poe, Mary Shelley, Nathaniel Hawthorne and Rudyard Kipling often lent their talents to those gift books, as did Sir Walter Scott and Lord Dunsany. Sir Arthur Conan Doyle made his contributions as well, and, in fact, debuted the character of Sherlock Holmes in a story for a Christmas annual.

So it's proven that there is a long-standing association between fictional ghost stories, and Christmas.

But what about *true* ghost stories?

As I researched material for this book, I found a number of factual ghost stories that were said to have taken place during the holidays or that were somehow connected to the Christmas holiday season. It's interesting to speculate as to why. Are we more aware of our spiritual natures at that time of year? Are deceased loved ones more apt to be on our minds when we are surrounded by the memory cues of custom and tradition?

Perhaps it has nothing to do with us at all. Perhaps it is more the choice of those souls who are returning. Many spirits who do come back do so with goodwill and heart-warming purpose. It seems appropriate that such benevolent entities would choose to undertake their missions during this particular time of year.

Of course, whether or not certain touching stories have actually taken place at Christmastime, the Christmas season certainly provides a most suitable backdrop for their retelling. And that raises the inevitable subject of the separation of fiction from fact.

Most storytellers will agree that a truly good tale contains one part truth and one part dramatic color. In this particular book, I have invented characters, relationships, dialogue and some background details—in order to protect the privacy of those who prefer to remain anonymous and to create a certain level of entertainment. The supernatural events within the stories, however, were presented to me as true. I have altered these details very little, in the interest of maintaining the appeal of such authentic accounts.

And they *are* appealing. If you dare to doubt it, please review your Victorian history. Anyone of that era would be pleased to tell you that it's not truly Christmas until the tree has been trimmed, the gifts have been wrapped and a ghost story has been told by the fireside.

So, Merry Christmas to all, and to all a good fright...

These are the spirits of the season...

Part 1

Gifts

"It is more blessed to give than to receive."

—Bible, Acts of the Apostles

Star Bright

The ornaments on the Christmas tree were old and cheap looking. Many had broken over the years and had been replaced by other small sets of baubles that didn't match. There were two different strings of lights, and the bulbs were of different styles. One string blinked; the other didn't. The angel that perched above the eclectic mess was missing a good deal of white nylon hair, which thematically complemented the tinsel rope, with its many bald patches.

Sharon could tell that Christi didn't care, though. Christi, who was still too young to compare her surroundings to the perfectly appointed homes that Sharon loved to look at in glossy magazines, thought that the tree was beautiful.

"It's so sparkly," she kept saying, with her five-year-old sense of wonder.

"It is, honey. We did a good job," replied Sharon. She put on a big smile and gave her little girl an enthusiastic high-five. Inside, she felt depression sinking into her bones. The Christmas tree that was lacking so many things was most notably lacking even a single festively wrapped gift beneath it.

Sharon turned out most of the lights in the small apartment, so that Christi could enjoy the full effect of the multicolored blinking bulbs. And she did enjoy it, completely. The child stood in the bathroom doorway, staring at the lights while she brushed her teeth. They cast a soft rainbow across her face as she sat on the living-room floor, putting on her pyjamas. As Sharon pulled out the sagging

sofa bed, where her daughter slept, Christi could barely contain her joy.

"I love this Christmas tree so, so, *so* much! If I wake up tonight, I won't be scared a bit, because I'll just look at all the pretty lights!"

"Oh, Christi," Sharon said. "We can't leave the lights turned on all night. It'll run up the bill, and we have to be careful."

"It won't cost very much," Christi declared, with total confidence.

"You have no idea how much anything costs," replied Sharon, sounding a little more brittle than she had intended.

It was true, though. They did have to be careful with money, and Christi *didn't* understand. Not that Sharon really wanted her to. A child of her age didn't need to know that there had been no financial support from her father since she was two, or that her mother's part-time paycheck barely covered the cost of essentials, let alone luxuries like Christmas gifts and all-night twinkling light shows.

It had been easier when Pearl was with them. But there was no point in dwelling upon that.

Pearl had been Sharon's grandmother, although being addressed as such was simply not her style. The one time Sharon had tested the waters with a tentative "Grandma..." Pearl had snapped her back in her predictable fashion.

"Girlie," she had said, "that's not my name. That's a *job description.*"

It was a job she took seriously. When Sharon had problems at home, which was often, Pearl provided sanctuary. When she got married, Pearl made the cake and the dress. And when Sharon was left devastated and bewildered after her husband ran off with a 19-year-old waitress, Pearl had been there to help pick up the pieces.

"Don't cry, honey," she had said, as she tapped half an inch of cigarette ash into a ceramic mermaid ashtray of her own creation. "There's a lid for every pot." Pearl was full of such homespun wisdom, ridiculous sayings that, strangely, seemed to help when they were delivered with such caring.

Eventually, it was Pearl who needed the help. She broke her arm one summer and caught pneumonia the following winter, and became too frail to manage on her own. She moved in with Sharon and Christi then, stuffing most of her curious old-lady possessions into the little apartment's single bedroom. Sharon and Christi shared the old sofa bed for the 18 months that Pearl lived with them. It was crowded, but none of them minded. Sharon was happy that Pearl hadn't been forced to move from her comfortably cluttered home to a sterile senior's complex.

Occasionally, Pearl had suggested that the senior's home might be a more practical solution.

"You don't need me here, getting in your way," she had said.

Sharon had refused to discuss it.

"I like having you around," she said. "Besides, Pearl, you'd wither in one of those places. After so many years, I know your style."

So Pearl stayed, and she entertained them, and she bought a few groceries and paid a bit toward the rent. Although Sharon's reasons for inviting the elderly woman into her home had been selfless, it did help to have someone sharing a bit of the financial burden. But then Pearl had died, in August, and Pearl's pension checks stopped coming in September. The money was missed a little, and Pearl was missed a lot.

There were little reminders of the woman everywhere. In the mornings, Sharon still brewed tea in Pearl's quirky pot, which was shaped like a cow. In the back of the bedroom closet were several of Pearl's more flamboyant outfits, the dresses upon which she had sewed feathers and sequins, creating garish patterns that were, in the eyes of the eccentric woman, beautiful. A glass bottle of Pearl's favorite lilac perfume sat on Sharon's dresser, and the apartment was still littered with the old woman's collection of bizarre figurines and handmade crafts. When Sharon had opened the box of Christmas ornaments, she even found Pearl's presence there. The woman had loved to dabble in oils, and one of her terrible, original paintings had been packed with the other seasonal decorations. At first, Sharon had wondered why, but when she lifted the painting out of the box and took a good look, she understood.

It was a likeness of the three wise men—actually, three murky, indistinguishable blots on the canvas—identifiable only because of the disproportionately huge, lemon yellow star that hung in the sky above them. Pearl's artistic vision had the wise men walking across a rolling expanse of neon-green grass, towing their gifts for the baby Jesus in a sturdy red wagon. They appeared more confused than wise as they traveled past the star, rather than toward it. Still, Pearl had obviously considered this one of her masterpieces, as she had gone to the trouble of placing it in a heavy plastic frame with a glass cover.

Sharon had been smiling with reminiscence, but had been about to put the painting back in the box when Christi had stopped her.

"Momma!" she had squealed. "Those are wise guys! We learned that at Bible Camp!"

And so, Pearl's depiction of Christi's "wise guys" had been hung dutifully on the wall behind the rocking chair, where it presided with gaudy authority over the living room.

Sharon stood beside it that night as she listened to Christi say her prayers.

"...and God bless everyone, even Pearl, up in heaven, and please could I have a 'Little Miss Magic Colors Jewelry Maker' for Christmas. Amen."

Sharon wasn't sure what to say.

"Christi—we don't ask God for Christmas presents," she finally stammered.

"Is that Santa Claus's job?" Christi asked. She wore an expression of severe concentration, as she tried to mentally navigate this complex hierarchy.

"Well, I suppose, yes."

"Okay." Christi slid off the sofa bed and was back on her knees in an instant. She folded her hands together and closed her eyes.

"Then, God, please let me go to the mall tomorrow where I can see Santa Claus and ask *him* for a 'Little Miss Magic Colors Jewelry Maker,'" she prayed. Satisfied then that she had taken care of business, Christi crawled back under the covers and closed her eyes.

"Goodnight, baby," Sharon whispered, as she kissed her daughter's forehead. Then she unplugged the lights on the tree and retreated to her bedroom.

Sharon usually read for a while after she tucked Christi in. Sometimes she carried their little portable television into the bedroom for a couple of hours of mindless entertainment. She knew that night, though, that neither activity would erase her gloom over not being able to buy Christi a proper Christmas present, so she simply shut off the lights, undressed, and slid beneath the covers. Before she closed her eyes, she offered her own prayer, of sorts.

"Pearl," she said, "I wish you could tell me what to do.

I could use the advice of a wise guy, or even a crazy old woman like you."

Then Sharon drifted off and did not wake until several hours later, when the light began to flash.

It was bright enough to invade her dreamless sleep and startle her to a sitting position.

"What is it?" Sharon mumbled. As she became a little more conscious, she knew what it had to be. Christi must have wakened, sometime in the night, and plugged the Christmas lights back in. In the complete darkness, the lights appeared to be more glaring. Sharon raised a hand to shield her eyes against the brightness as she swung her legs out from under the blankets. She was a little irritated at Christi, and a little surprised. The girl was not normally disobedient.

Once Sharon shuffled out to the living room, though, she could see that Christi had done nothing wrong. The child was sleeping soundly, sprawled kitty-corner across the sofa bed in a tangle of blankets. The tree stood in its corner, a silent, dark sentry. Whatever light had shone into Sharon's bedroom had not come from the twisted ropes of tiny light bulbs that had earlier been strung around its branches. It was actually impossible to say where the light *had* come from, because somewhere between the bedroom and living room, the brilliance had faded away.

Sharon scanned the apartment one more time. Finding nothing amiss, she turned and started back down the hall toward her bedroom.

Suddenly, the hall was filled with light, and Sharon's sharply defined shadow stretched out in front of her.

She spun around, trying to catch the light's source. At first, the glare was so blinding, Sharon had to squint until her eyes were nearly shut. After a moment, though, her vision adjusted to the point where she could see that the beam was coming from the glass front of Pearl's painting. Something from outside the living room window had to be hitting the surface just so, creating the intense reflection.

"Aha," Sharon said, softly. "The wise guys gotta go someplace else."

Re-hanging the picture was a job that would wait until morning, however. Sharon took the painting off the wall and laid it on the coffee table, ensuring that she wouldn't be bothered by the reflected light for the remainder of the night.

Once again, she made her way down the hallway. Once again, she stopped before turning into the bedroom.

It was as though someone had turned on a lamp behind her. Light filled the hallway, but it was indirect this time, not as harsh. Sharon turned around, not knowing what she would see.

She saw the painting, lying flat on the coffee table, emitting a brilliant, white beam skyward. Above it, on the cracked, plaster ceiling, the light formed a well-defined, five-point star.

"Oh, Pearl," Sharon breathed. Every hair on her body was standing at attention. Her feet felt leaden, weighted to the floor, but she forced them to take her back into the living room.

By the time Sharon was standing next to the painting, its mysterious light had begun to dim, a little. She watched in awe as it flickered and then extinguished, as though a battery had just gone dead. Sharon reached out tentatively and touched the glass cover, directly above the star. It had become just slightly warm.

Before her nerve left her, Sharon snatched up the painting and took it with her into the bedroom. She closed the door, turned on the light, and climbed into the middle of the bed. There, she sat cross-legged, holding Pearl's ugly little work of art by its spray-painted plastic frame.

There had to be a logical explanation, and Sharon meant to find it.

She ran her fingers lightly over the glass, looking for a warp or imperfection. She found none. She shook the frame, listening for the telltale rattle of a battery or wires. She heard nothing.

"That doesn't mean they're not there," she said to herself and began to push at the tiny metal tabs that held the back of the frame securely in place. Twice, she stopped to rub her hands vigorously on her pyjama legs. Her fingers were tingling, as though they had picked up some sort of strange static charge.

As Sharon loosened the cardboard backing of the frame, a vague hint of lilac wafted past her nostrils. When she turned the last tightly fastened tab, and the backing sprung up from the position in which it had been wedged, there was an overpowering burst of the scent. It was thick and choking enough to make Sharon cough, but still, she barely noticed. She was unable to take note of anything, other than what she saw lining the back of Pearl's painting.

Neatly taped together were rows and rows of 50-dollar bills.

Sharon began to tremble, and then she began to cry. In her usual, over-the-top style, Pearl had found a way to help her.

By the time Christi woke up, Sharon was scrambling eggs in the little galley kitchen.

"Get dressed, sleepy-head," Sharon told her. "We have a busy day ahead."

Christi rubbed her eyes and yawned.

"You *said* you wasn't going to work, today," she complained.

"I'm not," said Sharon, as she divided the eggs onto two plates and set them on the table. "But I recall hearing something from you about wanting to visit Santa Claus at the mall. And, while we're there, I thought we might have lunch, and do a little shopping."

Christi didn't need to be told twice. She ate her breakfast, dressed without being coaxed along, and washed her face and hands without being asked.

Sharon was equally eager. She put on her favorite outfit, and spent extra time and attention on her hair and makeup. She experienced a little thrill of excitement every time she thought of the cash that filled her wallet, and a warm swell of gratitude that came with knowing that the money would allow her to buy some of the things that her daughter would ask the mall Santa Claus for.

The picture frame had been holding more than $1000 in crisp, flat fifties. It was enough for Sharon to pay a few bills, buy them a nice Christmas, and even put a bit away for a rainy day.

"Get your coat on, Christi," Sharon called, as she fished some change out of her purse for the bus. "Your mitts and boots, too. If we hurry, we can catch the Number Five."

The apartment's front door buzzer sounded then, and Sharon experienced her only vaguely negative emotion of the morning. Whoever it was, was going to cause them to miss the next bus and put them 15 minutes behind. When she opened the door, however, she felt ashamed for having had the slightest of uncharitable thoughts. Standing there was a thin, stooped, old woman who lived on the first floor. She had been one of Pearl's closest friends.

"Hey, Vera!" Sharon said. "I haven't seen you for a while. Come on in."

Christi, who knew that the unexpected guest meant a delay, stopped trying to cram her right foot into her left boot. With a pout that she was wise enough to hide, she retreated into the living room.

Vera walked into the apartment, pulling her little folding shopping cart behind her. Into it, she had stuffed two cardboard cartons and a large brown paper bag.

"Well, I would have come by sooner, or had you down for a cup of coffee, but my bones were acting up. The cold, you know." Vera spotted Christi sitting on the sofa, then, and waved. "Hello, sweetheart," she warbled. "I see you way over there." Christi waved back, politely.

"Well, would you like some tea?" asked Sharon, and she set her purse on the ledge by the door, preparing to stay. Vera had always been kind to Pearl, looking in on her often, while Sharon was at work.

"No, no, I have Christmas baking to do, today. The first time I've felt up to it in weeks, so I'd best get to it. I just wanted to bring you these things, of Pearl's." She waved one arthritic hand vaguely in the direction of the shopping cart. "She asked me to store 'em in my extra closet—said that there was no room, up here. She meant for you to have 'em, though; you know, *after*. And I figured you might have room, now."

Vera turned around then, and started back out the door.

"Don't worry about the cart right now," she said. "I don't shop 'til Tuesday, when the specials come on. So, just bring it by before then, or give it to that nice maintenance man to bring down. He's the one who hauled it up here, for me, in the first place." Vera laughed at that, as though it was a great joke. Then she gave another little wave, and was gone.

Sharon looked at the clock. They had missed the Number Five, so there was no point in leaving the apartment for another 10 minutes, when the next bus would be nearly due. She eyed the cartons and bag in the little cart.

"Well, Christi-bell," she said, "let's see what treasures of Pearl's we have here."

She unfolded the top of the bag, and peered inside. Quickly, then, she opened the first cardboard carton, then lifted it out of the cart and opened the box that sat beneath it.

"Momma, what's wrong?" Christi asked, then declared, "Sumpin' smells like Pearl."

The room had filled with the thick, heady aroma of lilac perfume. Sharon was aware of it, but she was *more* aware of the static-y buzzing on her fingertips. She rubbed them against the rough weave of her sweater, trying to lose the sensation, as she stared at what Vera had just delivered to them.

Both boxes, and the paper bag, held several of Pearl's original paintings. Her favorites, one would have to assume, because each had been lovingly encased in an ornate plastic frame with a bulging cardboard backing. Sharon didn't have to pry them open to know that Pearl, who didn't have life insurance and had never believed in banks, had just left them a small fortune.

Sharon wiped carefully under her eyes, being careful to not smudge her mascara.

"Nothing's wrong, honey," she finally answered Christi. "It's just that these paintings remind me of Pearl."

"Maybe you would feel better if we put one up," the little girl suggested. "Maybe there, beside the wise guys." She pointed to the wall where Sharon had re-hung Pearl's Christmas star painting. There was room beside it for another.

"That's a great idea, Christi," Sharon said, and, together, they selected a cartoonish self-portrait of Pearl wearing a rhinestone tiara and a beaded satin bathrobe.

Sharon pounded a nail in the wall and centered the odd-looking, colorful picture upon it. After regarding the painting for a moment, however, Sharon took it down, and carried it into the kitchen. There, she peeled off its backing and stashed its bounty in the highest cupboard. Only then did she hang the painting back in the living room, because, as grateful as Sharon was for the gift, she had no wish to be awakened at midnight by the blinding flash of eerily illuminated rhinestones.

She knew that's what would happen.

After so many years, she knew Pearl's style.

A Ring from a Friend

"Ask Norman Taylor if I'll pass my history exam!"

"No, let's ask Norman Taylor if I'll get a wagon for my birthday!"

"I think before Norman Taylor leaves us, we should ask him which of you children neglected to take off your muddy shoes before walking all over my polished floor."

It was a happy scene. A large family, a crackling fire and a comfortably appointed, cheerful parlor. Outside the mellow warmth of the large home, it was damp and dark. The wind cried out and the water in the bucket that sat by the pump was capped with a thin disc of ice. It was a particularly unpleasant winter on Vancouver Island, but that bothered the family not a bit. They had found a game that amused them, long into the dark, cold nights, and they had met Norman Taylor.

Norman Taylor was a spirit, and the game they were playing was Ouija.

Though the family did not delve deeply into spiritualism, they found the Ouija board to be an entertaining distraction. The children loved to ask their "important" questions, and the spirits seemed happy to provide cryptic replies. One evening, when the family asked their spectral visitor to identify itself, the planchette spelled out the name "Norman Taylor." Norman must have felt welcomed, for he visited often after that. Eventually, he became the only spirit with whom the family communicated.

"Ask Norman Taylor..." began the youngest boy.

"Enough," said the father. "Each of us has had a turn, except Melissa. She has been waiting patiently, and *quietly,*

I might add." He cast a mockingly stern look at his sons. They simultaneously opened their mouths to protest, then snapped them shut, as their better judgment caught up with them.

"Melissa?" said the mother. "Do you have a question for Norman Taylor this evening?"

Melissa, the eldest, was a pretty, young woman just barely out of high school who tended to blush charmingly whenever eyes were upon her.

"I don't think so, Mother. That is, nothing comes to mind."

"Ask about that boy!" her younger sister urged. "The good-looking one, who's working as a clerk, down at the..."

"Margaret!" Melissa shot her sister an evil look. The color in her cheeks had gone from roses to fire. "I *said* I have nothing to ask!"

Apparently, however, the family's invisible guest did not agree, for as the sisters argued, and the brothers clamored for attention, the planchette began to scrape slowly across the wooden board.

"Oh, hurry, someone put their hands on!" said the mother. The girls quickly obeyed, resting their slim fingers lightly on the little heart-shaped object.

No clerk for M, Norman Taylor spelled out. Though she attempted to appear indifferent, a shadow of disappointment had fallen across Melissa's graceful features. The girl's dampened mood did not slow the movement of the planchette, however.

In three years time, began the longest message ever relayed by the spirit through the Ouija board. Norman Taylor told Melissa that, in the future, he would send a romantic friend to her from far away. She would recognize the man by a signet ring that he would one day place upon her finger. Their romance would be true, their life together long.

When the message was complete, the wooden planchette drifted across the board to the word *goodbye*. The girls sat back in their chairs, flexing the strained muscles of their hands, which they had held stiffly poised for the duration of the communication.

Margaret was the first to speak.

"That is *so* romantic," she breathed.

"Yes, it is, isn't it?" said Melissa. The brightness had returned to her eyes, and all thoughts of the good-looking clerk had vanished from her mind. The possibility of a handsome foreigner, assigned to her by the fates, was far more appealing.

"That was so sappy," said the boys, in chorus. They were cross that there had been no opportunity for their final questions.

"Don't worry," said their father, as he put the board away in its box. "Norman Taylor will be back again."

But, as it happened, that was the last time the family ever communicated with the spirit.

Soon, the breezes began to blow warm, and the icy gray melted out of the sky, and spring came to the island in a wash of lovely color and a waft of fresh scent. The badminton net was raised, the bicycles came out of the shed, and there were long walks past the neighborhood flower gardens to be taken. The Ouija board, that entertainment of the confining winter night, was put into storage.

The next winter was milder, perfect for ice-skating parties and hay rides. The board did not come out that year.

It was similarly ignored the winter after that.

By the time three years had passed, the Ouija board had long been forgotten, as had the messages and predictions of the faithful spirit who called himself Norman Taylor.

"If you keep kissing me like that, I'm apt to drop my parcels."

Melissa had grown into a woman. Though still a romantic, she had become more practical and less apt to flush crimson at the slightest hint of attention or impropriety. She put her suitor in place with a severe, if lovely, look.

"You shouldn't be carrying them anyway. Allow me."

The young man was as blonde and blue-eyed as was Melissa herself. He stood a head above her and had strong, broad shoulders, and they made a handsome couple as they walked along Victoria's busy downtown streets.

It was the holiday season, and shoppers were out in multitude. There were those who bustled along fretfully, brows furrowed and impossibly long lists in hand. There were those who had come for the atmosphere, and they took their time, stopping to admire the wreaths and ribbons that bloomed on every storefront and lamppost. Melissa and her gentleman kept to a pace that fell somewhere between those two groups. They were shopping, but in a leisurely fashion, pausing often to take in a charming window display or to say hello to an acquaintance.

They also stopped frequently to touch hands, or share some gesture of affection. They had been courting for several months. It was long enough for the two to feel a true bond, but not so long that the blossom of romance had begun to wilt. Quite the opposite had occurred: the fanciful setting of the holidays made the couple feel nearly giddy about their ardor. Whenever the fellow felt that they had some degree of privacy—in the back corner of a store, or when they were shielded by a passing carriage—he would take the opportunity to steal a quick kiss. As they turned a corner, and found themselves on a quiet, tree-lined avenue, he leaned over once more.

"Thomas!"

"Ah. Yes. The packages." Thomas took the carefully wrapped items out of Melissa's arms, balancing them amongst his own boxes and bags.

"Tell me again why it was necessary to nearly buy out the shops?" he asked.

"We're sort of having to double up," she explained. "Of course you bought a gift for your mother, but it was only appropriate that I should give her something as well. The same goes for your father, and your sister. And then you're buying for my family, in return..."

"It's gotten out of hand," Thomas grumbled, though he still wore an expression of good nature. "Next year, everyone gets one gift from us, as a couple."

Melissa said nothing, but smiled demurely. Inside, she savored the implication of his words.

They walked for a while in companionable silence, enjoying the slight chill of the air, and the sight of holly and ivy trimming each door along their way. Darkness was falling, and windows were illuminated with warm, inviting light from within. As the street lamps began to glow in soft response, Thomas turned to Melissa.

"I know your parents are expecting us," he said, "but can we stop, for just a moment? There's a bench just over there, in that private little park, and I would like very much to ask you something."

"Of course, Thomas," said Melissa. She pretended to look surprised, and even a little concerned.

Moments later, the mountain of packages and shopping bags had been settled at one end of the bench, and Melissa sat primly at the other. Thomas did not sit. Instead, he knelt before her.

"Melissa," he began, and his voice trembled slightly with nervousness, "you know how very much I've come to care about you. I think—that is, I hope—that you feel the same way toward me. I was going to wait until later—until I could get a proper ring—but the time just seems right, and you're so very...Oh, damn. Pardon me. I want to know if you'll be my wife, Melissa, and if you say yes, I have a temporary ring that I thought might do."

Thomas loosened his collar. Despite the cool December temperatures, he had begun to perspire.

"I am sorry," he said. "That wasn't the speech I had planned at all."

"It was fine, it was *fine*," said Melissa. "You are a wonderful, romantic man, and, yes, I will marry you!"

"You will. You will?" Thomas suffered a moment of incredulity, then began to laugh, with delight. He rose to his feet and swept Melissa into his arms.

"Marvelous! You'll never regret it, never!"

Together, they spun joyously in circles, laughing and embracing. When finally they slowed to a stop, Melissa waggled the fingers of her left hand, teasingly.

"I believe you said something about a ring?" she said.

"Oh, yes! It's temporary, as I said. My old school ring. We'll get something more appropriate, in time. Soon, that is. I promise." Thomas hunted though the pockets of his coat until, finally, he produced a small jeweler's box.

"Ah, here we are. Now if m'lady will again take a seat..." He gestured to the bench with a flourish.

"My pleasure!" Melissa sat down, employing comparable theatrics.

Thomas knelt before her, once more, and his broad smile softened into an expression of tenderness.

"I do love you, Melissa," he said. "Thank you for saying 'yes.'" With that, he took the small gold ring from the box, and placed it upon her finger.

Melissa looked at the ring, and her face changed. Her eyes narrowed, and her brow furrowed, as she attempted to knit together the elusive fragments of a lost memory.

"What is it?" Thomas asked. "You despise the ring, don't you. You needn't wear it, if you feel that way, Melissa. I promise you that, soon, I'll have a real engagement ring for you."

"No, it's not that..." Melissa spoke vaguely, as she tried to remember.

Then, it all came back.

"Norman Taylor!" she shouted, and jumped off the bench. "Norman Taylor told me about this signet ring! He told me about you, too, but I'd forgotten until just now!"

"I don't understand." Thomas was standing again, and had taken a step back. His face had grown pale, and serious. "How did you know about that? How did you know *Norman Taylor?*"

Melissa took one look at Thomas's face, and was pulled back to the present.

"Oh, no, it wasn't like that," she explained, attempting to assuage the jealousy that she imagined she saw in Thomas. "I didn't really know him, not the way you think..."

Thomas shook his head, violently.

"No, Melissa. I mean, I went to *school* with Norman Taylor. In Australia, when I was away for all those years."

"Oh," said Melissa, a trifle embarrassed at the misunderstanding. "Well, then, it could hardly have been the same 'Norman Taylor' that we each knew," she said.

Thomas considered that, and the intense set of his features began to soften.

"No," he admitted. "Of course not. I'm sorry, it's just that Norman was my best friend, there. I still get upset when I think about him."

"Why?"

"Well," Thomas said, and after a moment's hesitation, he confessed. "He died, you see. Years ago. The two of us, we were up on the roof of the school, getting into a bit of mischief. We were doing nothing terribly wrong, but Norman lost his footing, and he fell. He broke his neck. I felt quite guilty—I still do, to tell the truth—because we had sworn to look out for one another. We were both a long way from home, where it's good to have a friend in your corner."

Thomas looked at Melissa, then, and offered her a sad smile. "I would have liked for Norman Taylor to meet you," he said. "I know he would have approved."

Melissa was quiet, for a moment. Then, showing wisdom and discretion that would serve her well in all the years of marriage that lay ahead, she simply nodded, and took Thomas's hand in her own.

"I would have liked that, too," was all she said.

The rest of the story, she felt, was best saved for another day and time.

The Savior at Sea

"Will you look now, you've gotten us killed."

Peter did have to admit that it looked bad. It had been five days since he and his friend, Eric, had sailed from San Francisco. The tramp steamer upon which they had been working had just gone down in flames. The debris that bobbed in the waves around them included a good number of dead bodies, and there was not a lifeboat or a piece of land to be seen.

Still, one had to stand up for one's self.

"It wasn't all my fault," he said to Eric. "I may have found us the jobs, but you were the one griping that you had no money to get home for Christmas. I was only trying to *help*."

"And will this help?" asked Eric. "Does it look like I'm going to get to kiss my girl under the mistletoe as a bloated, kelp-ensnared, shark-ravaged, bloody, *corpse?*"

Peter had known Eric for a long time, and he knew when it was time to change the subject.

"At least we caught something good to hang on to," he said, patting the ragged board to which they both clung for their very survival. "And you never know when someone might happen along."

"Oh, yes! I'd say there's such a good chance of that, let's not jump at the first opportunity that comes our way. Let's hold out for a yacht, what do you say? Or maybe a cruise ship; something with a pool and a bar, hmm?"

"You don't have to make fun of me," pouted Peter, and spit out a mouthful of bitter seawater.

"Peter!" shouted Eric. "*It's all I have left!*"

The two bobbed along in silence for an hour or so then. The sun rose, high in the sky above them, and glared down mercilessly.

"I don't know if I'm more thirsty, or more tired," complained Peter. "This is rough, all this floating. You wouldn't think so, to watch it. It looks like the water does all the work, but really..."

"Shut up, Peter." When Eric spoke, his tongue felt thick. His lips were cracked and dry, and when he licked them, he tasted nothing but salt. Every wave that lapped over him bathed him in salt, which the sun and wind then forced into his pores.

"It's like being marinated to death," he muttered.

"You sound delirious," Peter nodded solemnly. He knew all about delirium at sea. The old deck hand who had accidentally started the fire in the galley had been telling him stories. First a fellow got light-headed, and then a bit dizzy, the way Peter had been feeling all morning. Then, you started to see things. Mirages—things that you wanted to see, like a beautiful woman or a rescue vessel. Sometimes the images would make no sense, like the old man that Peter could see, rowing his way toward them. *Imagine—a rowboat, in the middle of the Pacific Ocean,* Peter thought. The thought made him laugh and, as he did, a little wave lapped over the board and hit him squarely in the face. He choked on most of the water, spit the rest out, and reminded himself for the tenth time that day to keep his mouth closed.

"Whasso funny," slurred Eric. He hated to be excluded from a joke. It always made him suspicious.

"Nothing. I mean, it's just something in my head, Eric.

I thought I saw...I thought I saw..." Peter was hit with a fit of weak giggles, every time he tried to say it.

"Never mind what you thought you saw, you nit," said Eric. He was suddenly alert, shielding his eyes with one hand, and staring at the horizon. "Let me tell you what *I* see. It's a boat—someone in a rowboat!" He began to laugh. "Despite your best efforts to destroy us, Peter, we are *saved!*"

"But that doesn't make any sense..." Peter's features twisted into an expression of supreme confusion.

"Fine. When the boat gets here, you can just tell the guy, 'Sorry, sailor, but you don't make *sense*, so I'm just going to stay here with my floating board.' But me, I'm going for a ride. I'm going home for Christmas."

Eric started to wave, then, and used the last of his energy to call out.

"Hey! Buddy! We're over here!"

The little boat turned, and began to drift toward Peter and Eric. The man at the oars did not appear to be applying much effort, but the boat seemed to reach them in a matter of seconds, skimming smoothly over the choppy water. Sitting in the little craft was a weathered sailor. His face was a mask of sorrow, and he stared vacantly ahead, past Peter and Eric and their bobbing piece of wood.

"Thank God, you found us!" panted Eric. "We thought we were done for!"

"I've been a fool," the man said, to no one in particular.

"Yeah, well, you *could* have gotten here a little earlier, but we're so happy to see you, we'll just let bygones be bygones, okay? Okay. Can you help us aboard? We're a little weak, here."

The strange sailor reached out, over the edge of the boat. Instead of grasping Eric's outstretched hand, though, the man plucked a large fish out of the water, as if by magic. In one swift motion, he tore it in two, and handed one half to each man.

"Drink the water from its innards," he instructed, solemnly. "Chew its flesh, for sustenance."

Peter and Eric looked at the raw, mangled fish that they held in their hands. Then they looked at each other.

"What do I care?" said Peter. "I'm hallucinating this, anyway."

Both men did as the sailor told them. After a while, much to their surprise, they felt noticeably revived.

"I think I can climb aboard, now," announced Eric. He let go of the board, grasped the side of the rowboat, and pulled himself over. Once settled in the boat, he reached out toward Peter.

"Come on," he said. "Join the party, what do you say?"

"It's an illusion," Peter maintained. "But, what the heck." He took Eric's hand and climbed aboard.

The sailor began to ply the oars then, and the three men floated away from the debris of the steamer. They remained at sea for the rest of the day.

Most of the time, the group was silent. Occasionally, Peter or Eric would try to talk to the sailor. He seldom answered them at all, and never answered them directly.

"You're not a talker, are you?" Eric asked, at one point.

"I've been a fool," mourned the sailor.

"Like I said, don't beat yourself up," said Eric, then let the attempted conversation drop.

As the sun set, the little rowboat came to rest on the shore of a tiny, deserted island. Though it was little more than a bit of exposed rock, it gave them a dry place to spend the night. Peter and Eric slept away their exhaustion, and woke early to a distressing sight.

The sailor was preparing to leave without them.

"Wait a minute!" cried Eric, as he stumbled across the rocks to the water's edge. "You can't leave without us!"

"He's not really leaving," said Peter, who had finally come to believe that the man was not just a figment of his weary mind. "You're not really leaving, are you?" He sat up and rubbed his eyes.

"I must leave, for I've acted very foolishly. But first,

I want to tell you my wife's address, and the number of a safety deposit box, in San Francisco." The sailor gave them the information, and then added, "The key for the box is in a shed, behind my wife's house. I want my wife to have everything that's in that box."

"Yeah," said Eric. "We'd love to help. But that's going to be hard if we're reduced to being gull food on a rock!"

"I'll send help," promised the sailor. "You'll be home for Christmas Eve." He pushed on the oars then, and the boat was suddenly moving. By the time Eric splashed out into the water after it, it had somehow sped a great distance away.

"He didn't leave?" asked Peter, who was still trying to make sense of the situation. "Not really?"

But the sailor had left, and Eric and Peter spent the next several hours contemplating death on a rock, as opposed to death at sea.

"I'll never forgive you," Eric hissed, at one point. "If we meet a thousand ways, in a thousand different lifetimes, I will always remember, on some level, that you were my ruination."

"It's not healthy to hold a grudge," Peter said. "My mother always used to say 'hate corrodes the vessel that holds it.'"

"Your mother was a..."

"What's that noise?"

Both men fell silent, trying to identify the steadily increasing drone. Eric's eyes suddenly grew wide.

"That's a plane! An airplane engine!" He scrambled out from the sheltered spot where he had been lying.

"We're here!" he shouted, feebly, waving his arms.

"They'll never see us, Eric," moaned Peter. "Save your energy."

"They'll never see us? They'll *never see us?* What's that, then?" Eric pointed to the sky.

Peter rolled over and looked. The plane's cargo hold was open, and a package was falling toward them. It hit its mark, directly in the center of the barren outcropping of rock. The airplane banked then, carving a slow semi-circle in the cloudless sky. Once it was facing the direction from which it had come, it flew away.

The package held water, food and a brief, spirit-lifting message.

"*SHIP ON WAY,*" it read.

"The three most beautiful words in the English language," said Eric, as he tore into a package of chocolate.

Peter did have to admit that it looked good.

The Coast Guard rescued the men on the very next morning. Peter and Eric were told that their location had been reported by an odd-mannered fellow in a rowboat. The sailor had kept his promise, and now it was time for the two friends to keep theirs.

"You're being real thoughtful, Eric. Pardon my saying so, but I didn't expect it."

It was Christmas Eve, and Peter and Eric were walking through the streets of San Francisco, searching for the house address that the sailor had given them.

"Well, the kind of thing we just went through— it changes a man, you know. I'm not as selfish as I was last week, Peter. Last week, I would have been on my way home. But today—today, I'm thinking that the old sailor's wife might be expecting that safety deposit box key in time for Christmas. And, if there's a little payment for delivering the message, well, that wouldn't be so bad, now, would it?"

"Well, no. Although, theoretically, goodness is supposed to be its own reward."

"Theory rarely applies in life," said Eric. "Here we are."

The house was a shabby bungalow with cracked Spanish stucco and curling shingles. A little wreath hung crookedly on the front door, and a jolly, plastic Santa Claus, badly faded by the sun, had been propped beneath the mailbox. The cement-block sidewalk that led to the front door branched out around the side of the house, into the back yard. There was only a short picket fence enclosing the garden there.

"There's the shed," said Eric. "I think it would be a better surprise if we just got the key, first, and gave it to the woman."

Peter could think of no reason to object, so the two friends slipped quietly around the house and opened the little shed.

The key was exactly where the sailor had said it would be.

"This is interesting, you know," mused Eric. "We have the key, and we know the number of the safety deposit box. There are those who would call us foolish for handing over such a thing."

Peter looked at his friend with genuine alarm.

"Eric," he said, "you're not thinking of *keeping* the key? Tell me that, on Christmas Eve, of all nights, you're not thinking of stealing from the wife of the man who saved our lives?"

"Would it be our fault for 'misappropriating,' or his fault for trusting two perfect strangers with such important business?" Eric raised an eyebrow.

Peter paused for only a moment.

"No!" he said. "No! No! I'm not going to let you confuse me about this! Keeping that key would be *wrong*. Giving it to that woman, in there—that woman, who is alone for Christmas—that is the *right* thing to do. Check your conscience, Eric," he begged. "Try to imagine the sailor's wife, in her little house, there, with no presents under the tree, and no turkey in the oven. Now imagine her joy, and her gratitude, when you hand her that key, and give her that message from her husband! Picture the tears in her eyes, as she thanks you for your kindness! Let *that* be your reward, Eric! Let *that* be your bounty!"

"Let that be my *bounty?*" Eric said, as he made a sour face.

Peter nodded.

"Well, if it'll get you to shut up," Eric sighed. "That's probably worth more than whatever's in the box. And, anyway, I was only speaking theoretically."

"Theory rarely applies in life," reminded Peter. Eric shot him a warning look. "I'll be quiet, now," Peter promised, and made a zipping motion across his lips.

They knocked on the front door. After a minute, it was opened by a woman in hair curlers and a worn bathrobe. A cigarette dangled from her lips, and she didn't bother to remove it when she said, "Help you boys?"

Eric stepped forward.

"Actually, ma'am, we're here to help you," he said.

"That so?" The woman struck a defiant pose, with one hand on her hip. With the other hand, she finally plucked the cigarette out of her mouth, and coughed out a cloud of smoke.

Eric coughed a little himself, and continued.

"We have a message for you," he said. "A message from your husband."

The woman laughed a little.

"Oh, honey," she said. "I don't think so. The old man's dead."

Eric and Peter looked at each other.

"But this is..." Peter rattled off the address which they had been given by the sailor.

"Sure, that's my address," said the woman, "but my husband got drunk and fell off a ship eight years ago. Stupid fool."

"I don't get this," Eric persisted. "It doesn't make sense." He told the woman the story of their rescue. "So, you see," he concluded, "we *talked* to him. And he gave us this safety deposit box number, and told us to give this key to you!" He held up the key and a piece of paper upon which they had written the number.

The woman's face changed. Sudden interest animated her features; her eyes widened and her jaw dropped.

"Gimme that!" she said, and snatched the key and the paper from Eric's hands. "I don't believe it!" she marveled, as she looked the items over. "After all these years, the old bastard finally came through!" She let loose a rasping laugh.

"Boys, I always knew there was a few thousand stashed away in a safety deposit box at the bank. But Wilf—that was my old man's name, God rest his cantankerous soul— he never told me where he kept the key. I thought it was down at the bottom of the ocean, with his bones. But lookie-here." She turned the silver key from side to side, admiringly.

"You boys have a good Christmas," she said, then, and began to close the door.

Eric put out his hand to hold it open.

"Wait a minute!" he protested. "Is that it? No thanks? No dewy-eyed gratitude? No rewarding story about how we've saved your children from going hungry on Christmas day?"

The woman looked confused.

"I only got one kid," she said. "He runs a bowling alley in Dubuque."

Eric looked at Peter in exasperation. Peter shook his head and shrugged apologetically.

Eric began to knead the tense spot between his eyebrows.

"Okay, forget all that," he said to the woman. "But how about a little something for our trouble, huh? It's Christmas Eve, and instead of going home, we came here, to make this delivery to you. Shouldn't there be something in it for us?"

The woman appeared to consider his argument. After a moment, she spoke.

"Lemme see if I got this right: the 'ghost' of my idiot husband just kept you two from becoming fish food. That the basic story?"

Eric and Peter nodded their agreement.

The woman shrugged.

"Then I'd say you got yours. Merry Christmas, fellas!"

She slammed the door hard enough to knock the crooked wreath a little more off-kilter, and was gone.

Eric and Peter actually remained standing on the stoop for a few moments, so great was their disbelief. Eventually, they realized that the woman had retreated for good, and they turned and left.

It was a warm evening, and there were groups of people out caroling on every street. Peter found their festive cheer infectious.

"You know," he finally said to Eric, "that woman was right. We only did a small errand for the sailor, but he gave us the greatest gift that anyone can give. He gave us our lives!"

Eric refused to be mollified.

"I swear, Peter," he said, through clenched teeth, "not another freaking word. What I want for Christmas, this year, is for you to shut your mouth for 24 hours. That would be a supreme gift, and you don't even have to wrap it."

Peter nodded, genially. After a few minutes of silence, he turned to Eric.

"You want to get a turkey sandwich?" he asked.

There was pause, then Eric answered.

"Yeah. You can *buy* me a turkey sandwich," he said. "And pie."

"And then we're even?" Peter confirmed.

Eric spun around to face him.

"No, we're not 'even,' Peter! Not unless you can find me a turkey sandwich that's worth *thousands* of dollars! We are a *loooooong* way from even!"

Eric saw the wounded expression on his friend's face then, and he felt a small stab of guilt. He sighed.

"Okay," he conceded. "We won't be even, but it'll be a start."

Peter smiled. He fell into step beside Eric again, and began to whistle in tune with the closest group of carolers.

A start was good.

Peter did have to admit that it looked good.

The Twelve Days

On the gray December 14th when Harold and Jackie moved into the two-bedroom ground-floor suite of the apartment complex, Harold stood out on the front stoop and marveled at how his life had come to be defined by numbers.

It was the first day in the new apartment. It was the third new apartment in four years. The three moves had been necessary because of as many changes in teaching jobs. The number of dollars left in the savings account was 214, which was bad news because 300 was the approximate number of miles past when the hatchback should have had a full tune-up. Two was how many times Harold had awakened in a sweat the previous night, thinking of the new class he would have to face come January. And then there were the heaviest numbers on Harold's mind: he knew that in 11 days, he faced the fifth anniversary of Christopher's death. All of these things contributed to the fact that Harold was about to have his 18th cigarette of the day, before he even had his lunch.

This particular apartment did have a good stoop, he had to admit. There were broad, concrete steps that led to a generous landing in front of double doors. Running along the sides were solid railings that were wide enough to sit on, if a guy wanted to hang out for a while. That was conceivable, because the view wasn't terrible. The eight walk-up buildings had been arranged around a circular common area, a big patch of grass where folks could pull out a lawn chair and kids could play. Not that there were

any kids playing outside on that day. The temperature had dipped 15 degrees overnight, and the wind had started to sting. Even Harold, who approved so wholeheartedly of the stoop, only planned to be out on it for as long as it took him to finish his cigarette.

Jackie was merciless when it came to smoking. She wouldn't allow it inside the apartment, even on the most bitter winter days. Harold didn't blame her. He had actually been a reformed smoker for more than a decade, up until his life had begun to consist of a series of stressful changes.

He had begun to need a little something, then; a little, white, filter-tipped crutch to get through the days. And so, he had become expert in the matter of comfortable front stoops.

Harold finished his cigarette, crushed it against the sole of his shoe and pocketed the butt. He pulled open one of the heavy front doors and turned to take one last look around his new environment. That was the first time he saw the kid.

He was standing in the middle of the common area, a little boy of about six or seven. In his thin cargo pants, running shoes, and light, nylon windbreaker, he was badly underdressed for the weather. The cold didn't seem to be bothering him, though. He wasn't shivering or clutching his jacket tightly around him or trying to bury his ears in his shoulders the way Harold had seen kids in the school-yard do. He was standing calmly and still, staring at Harold with large, brown eyes from beneath a mass of kinky, dark hair. When he saw that Harold was staring back, he raised one hand in a friendly, if tentative, salute.

Harold waved back, and the kid smiled.

As he pulled the front door to the apartment building closed behind him, Harold looked back out through its warped half-moon–shaped window.

A rogue sheet of newspaper was blowing across the dead, brown grass of the common area. A few flakes of snow were beginning to ride the wind. But the kid had gone, back inside where it was warm, Harold supposed.

Harold returned to the chore of unpacking boxes and told Jackie his minor bit of news.

"I think I met one of our neighbors," he said.

Two days later, the unpacking was complete, and the weather changed. A chinook blew in, bringing temperatures so mild that the few patches of icy snow that had been around began to melt. Harold, who had no job to go to until the new semester began in January, took advantage of the balmy conditions. He sat out on the stoop for long periods that day, enjoying the soft, warm air on his face.

It was on his second outing that he saw the kid again. Harold had just lit a cigarette and had taken his eyes off the scenery for only a moment as he put his lighter back in his jacket pocket. When he looked up, the boy was standing there.

He was closer that time, shuffling his feet at the edge of the common area that was closest to the building that Harold and Jackie lived in. He wore the same outfit that he had had on the day that they had moved in, and that made Harold smile. *That's his uniform*, he thought. He had been in the kid business long enough to know that they often had a favorite outfit that their parents practically had to peel off of them on laundry day.

"Hi, buddy," Harold said to the kid, and gave him a wave.

It was all the encouragement the boy needed. He came over to the stoop and sat down on the bottom step, opposite Harold.

"Actually," the boy said, "my name's not 'buddy.' It's Charles Laffin."

"Oh," Harold said. "Sorry about that, Charles Laffin. My name's Harold."

"Did you just move here?" Charles asked.

"Yup. Two days ago. That's my apartment, right there,"

said Harold, and he pointed to his living room window, which was to the right of the entrance.

"You don't got any Christmas decorations in your window," noted Charles. "How come?"

"Well," Harold explained, "we did *just* move in. And, you know, my wife and I—we don't really 'do' Christmas."

Charles laughed.

"Christmas isn't somethin' you *do*," he said. "Christmas is somethin' that just *is!*"

"Well, that's a good point, Charles," Harold said. "I'll have to think about that."

I'll have to think about that was Harold's greatest diversionary tactic. It was something that he often said to his students; a lie, meant to appease them until such time that they forgot about whatever important issue they had brought to Harold's attention. Usually, it worked.

The next day, when Harold walked out the front doors with his cigarettes in one hand and his morning coffee in the other, he found that such evasiveness did not work on Charles Laffin.

"You *still* got no decorations up. Dint you say you were goin' to think about it?"

Charles was already seated on the steps. Harold felt as though he had been ambushed.

"Well, yeah," he said, as he eased himself down on the top step. Then he lit his cigarette and told another lie. "I *did* think about it Charles, but the truth is, I just don't like Christmas decorations very much."

Charles looked at Harold as though he was some alien form of life.

"*Everybody* likes Christmas decorations," he said. "I do. I like everything about Christmas."

"Everything, huh? Like what?" asked Harold.

Charles ticked things off, one by one, on his fingers.

"I like the pictures on the Christmas cards, and I like the special TV shows, and I like the presents, and the candy. I like making snowmen, but there's not enough snow, right now. I like the holiday from school, too."

"I like that one myself," Harold laughed, exhaling little puffs of smoke.

"And I like the songs, too. You know any Christmas songs?" Charles asked.

"Gee, I doubt it. How 'bout you?"

"We learned 'Away in a Manger' at Sunday school. That's a good song. You want me to sing it?"

Harold panicked.

"You know, I have to get going right now. But maybe another time," he said. Then he gathered his things and retreated into the building.

He spent the rest of that day inside the apartment, watching television. The nicotine cravings were awful, but that was easier to cope with than the memory of Christopher in a shepherd's costume, singing out of key at his first-grade Christmas concert.

Harold felt bad about running away from Charles. The next day, every time he went out on the stoop, he scanned the common area, hoping to see him. Harold even took a little walk around the perimeter of the complex, thinking that he might spot the boy playing behind his own building, or on the swings with some neighbor kids. There were a couple of separate groups of children, shuffling around on the playground in an aimless fashion, but there was no sign of Charles.

Harold was disappointed—it actually surprised him *how* disappointed he was—but thought that the boy was likely playing indoors. The weather had turned colder, again; not at all suitable for a little guy whose uniform didn't allow for winter temperatures.

The day after that was even colder, though, and there was Charles Laffin again, standing in the common area in his ridiculously light clothing. Harold, who was shivering in his wool hat and down-filled jacket, waved him over.

"Hey, Charles!" he said. "Aren't you *cold?*"

The boy shook his head, and his wild hair bounced to the beat.

"I feel fine," he said. Then, "Whatcha got there?"

"Mail," said Harold. He had met the postal carrier on his way out of the apartment. "Let's see what we have here. Bill. Bill. 'Occupant.' Big surprise—bill."

Then Harold saw something that caused him to brighten.

"Hey, come here, Charles!" he said. "This might be something you'll like."

Harold tore open the envelope with its holly-and-ivy stencil, and handed the Christmas card that was inside to Charles.

"You said you like these, right? You like the pictures?"

"Yeah," said Charles, as he traced his fingers over the Norman Rockwell reproduction on the front of the card. "This is a nice one. Who's it from?"

"My old bank," explained Harold. "It's highly personal. You can keep it, if you like."

"Thanks," said Charles, and slipped the card inside his jacket. He looked at the envelope then, and reached over to touch its forwarding-address sticker.

"When my aunt moved in with us, she got letters like that, for a while," he said. Then he frowned, as if trying to remember something, and asked Harold, "Where did you live before?"

"Oh," Harold hesitated. "Lots of places. A different place, every year, lately."

"How come you move around, so much?"

"I like fresh scenery."

"You not on the run?"

"The run?"

"Like bad guys. On the lam. Runnin' away from cops and stuff."

"Oh." Harold thought about it for a moment. "Well," he finally said to Charles, "I'm not a bad guy, and the cops don't care about me. But, I might be running away a little bit."

"Okay." Charles seemed unconcerned.

The two sat in silence for a minute or two, then. Harold watched his breath turn to fog in the icy air, and thought that despite his warm layers, he would have to get inside, soon.

Charles, who didn't appear to be the least bit distracted by the cold, broke the silence.

"My gramma has a sayin' about runnin' away," he said.

"She does, eh?"

"Yeah—she says 'you can't run away from your feet.' You know what that means?" Charles asked.

Harold took a moment to answer.

"Well," he finally said, "I guess it means that you can't escape something if it's a part of you."

Charles put his hands in his wooly hair, as though squeezing his brain would actually help him comprehend.

"Oh, man," he said, "I don't get that."

Harold thought about it for a little while, and then told him, "I do."

That night after dinner, Jackie complained to Harold that he was even less talkative than usual, and that if the television was to be her only companion, she was going to go ahead and spring for cable. Harold said that he wasn't meaning to ignore her; he was just doing some thinking.

In the end, he bundled up in his winter gear once more, so that he could sit outside on the stoop and have a bit of peace and quiet. While he was out there, he noticed a dark rectangle jutting out a bit from the second step. Harold picked it up and turned it over. The light over the door reflected off foil letters that read "Merry Christmas from the 'Friendly' Bank."

Harold shook his head, and smiled.

Must've slipped out of his jacket, he thought, although he had seen Charles zip it up tightly.

When Harold woke up on the morning of the 20th, he felt a little better. It was as if he had finally digested a meal that had been weighing heavily in his gut.

"We've been here a week," he said to Jackie, as he looked at the calendar. "I think I'm settling in. It's starting to feel a little bit like home."

"Shall I start to pack, then?" Jackie deadpanned.

"Ha, ha," said Harold, and grabbed his coat off the rack by the door.

"Going out front?" asked Jackie.

Harold paused for a moment.

"A little farther, actually," he said. "I think I'll go to the mall."

By the time Harold left the mall, he had lightened their savings account by $43. On the way home, he noticed that something else—some inscrutable thing—seemed lighter, as well. He actually caught himself whistling along with a Christmas carol on the car's AM radio.

When he got home, he grabbed a roll of packing tape out of the kitchen junk drawer, and took his purchase out of the bag.

"What have you there?" asked Jackie, peering over his shoulder.

"Surprise for my new friend," said Harold, and went to work.

That afternoon, he sat on the front stoop, smoking cigarettes and drinking coffee until Charles Laffin finally appeared.

Harold's head had been tilted back as he drained the very last drops of his decaf. When he had leaned forward again and lowered the mug, Charles was standing there.

It was sudden enough to make Harold jump.

"Whoa! You know how to sneak up on a guy, Charles."

"I got quiet shoes, I guess," the boy said. "Were you waitin' for me?"

"Yes, I was," nodded Harold. "Got a surprise for you. Now, you have to wait right here, okay?"

"Okay," said Charles. "I like surprises."

Harold ran inside then, through the double doors and then into his own apartment. Once there, he pulled back the sheer curtains that covered his front window, and looked out at the front stoop.

For a moment, his heart sank. He could see no one on the steps or the broad landing, and he thought that Charles Laffin had left. But he was wrong—the boy was there, leaning patiently against the railing. He had obviously ducked down, for a moment—to tie a shoelace, or pick up a pebble—and then reappeared in the sliver of time that it had taken Harold to blink.

Harold knocked on the windowpane. Charles looked up. He squinted briefly at the reflection on the glass, then saw past it to Harold. He waved, and Harold waved back. Then, Harold plugged in the extension cord.

It was as though the power surged directly to the boy's face.

His eyes widened, and his mouth formed a perfect "O." Then he broke into a smile, and he waved so hard at Harold, it appeared that his arm was about to take flight.

Harold walked back out of the building, and joined his young friend.

"Do you like it?" he asked, although he didn't have to.

"It's the best of anybody's!" Charles said. "It's beautiful!" He seemed unable to look away from the window, and what Harold had created there.

In small, twinkling, red and green lights, he had written

the words *Merry Christmas.* Beneath it, in blue, was the blinking script that read *Charles.*

"Well, hey," said Harold, and he found himself a little embarrassed. "You're my first pal in the neighborhood, and you said you liked Christmas lights, so..."

And then Charles turned to face Harold.

"Did your little boy like Christmas lights?" he asked.

Harold's stomach knotted.

"How did you know I had a little boy?" he said.

"You told me, I guess," Charles answered. Then, more confidently, "You told me."

There was a span of silence. The two stood in front of the window with Charles' name flashing against the approaching twilight. Finally, Harold decided that he would just answer the question.

"Yeah," he said. "He liked 'em."

"How 'bout Christmas trees?"

"Sure. He liked Christmas trees a lot."

"Then you should get one, I think." said Charles. "That'd be good. You did a *real* good job on this," he complimented Harold once more.

Then, he raised his hand in a small wave and was gone. Harold was transfixed by the window and forgot to turn around to see what building Charles walked into.

Whichever one it was, Harold hoped that Charles had a good view of his name, in lights.

The next day, Harold didn't see Charles Laffin, but he thought about him. Finally, he asked a question of Jackie.

"Did you mention anything about Christopher to that little kid named Charles who hangs around here?" he said.

Jackie tried to hide her surprise. She was unaccustomed to hearing Harold mention Christopher's name.

"Uh, no," she said. "How could I? I've never even seen this little friend of yours."

"Huh," said Harold. "Hmm."

He resolved to ask Charles about it again, when he saw him. But he didn't see him all that day, or the next.

On the 23rd, Harold took another few dollars out of the dwindling savings account, and drove to the nearest tree lot.

"There's not much left," said the vendor.

"That's okay," said Harold. "It doesn't have to be perfect."

And it wasn't. The tree that Harold ended up tying to the hatchback was short, and scrawny, and already beginning to drop needles. But it was good *enough*, and it wasn't like it had a hard act to follow.

"A *tree?*" said Jackie, when Harold hauled it through the front door. She nearly dropped the book she had been reading.

"Yeah, a tree," said Harold. Once he actually had it in the apartment, though, he began to feel a little impulsive and foolish.

"You know, I wasn't really thinking. I don't suppose we have the ornaments, anymore," he said.

"We'll make some," said Jackie, and ran into the other rooms to gather scissors, and paper, and anything that could possibly pass for a craft material.

Three hours later, the runty tree was resplendent in baubles made of colored paper, yarn and tinfoil. A flashlight, strategically placed upon the mantle, reflected off the foil and provided the illusion of lights.

Harold and Jackie lay entwined on the sofa, basking in the beauty of their creation.

"It may just be the best Christmas tree in the city," said Jackie, and Harold had to agree.

Before he went to bed that night, he put on his coat and wandered out in front of the building. It was past bedtime for most kids, but he had a strong hunch that he would find Charles there, or that Charles would find him.

He was right.

The boy was standing at the edge of the common area, staring at the decorated tree in the window.

"You did a real nice Christmas tree," he said. His arms were folded across his chest as he nodded his approval, and he looked like some 60-year-old sidewalk foreman.

"Thanks, Charles. We think it's nice, too. Me and Jackie, that is."

"So you're gonna 'do' Christmas now?" the boy asked with a sly smile.

Harold laughed out loud.

"Yeah. Well. I guess were already 'doing' it, aren't we?"

"Yup." Then, out of left field, Charles hit Harold with the question.

"So, how did your little boy die?"

Harold felt unusually capable of handling it.

"He was sick," he said. "Really sick, you know. He had leukemia. And, after a while, he got too sick to go on."

"When did it happen?" asked Charles. He was still staring at the tree.

"About five years ago. Almost five years ago." Harold had a crazy urge to say *let me just check my watch*. The anniversary, which had been simmering on a back burner in his mind, was creeping up.

"Well," said Charles, "I *know* he likes the tree." Then he raised one hand in his customary little wave, and began to walk away.

When Harold turned around, he was gone.

Snow had begun to fall, and as he walked back toward the apartment, Harold gazed at his own living room window with its twinkling holiday greeting, and its makeshift tree, and he quoted his wife.

"Best in the whole city," he said to himself, before he walked back inside.

December 24th dawned with a fresh blanket of snow.

Harold awoke, thinking of Christopher, as he did every year on that date. He felt sadness, too, as he did every year; but it seemed, somehow, that the razor's edge had been removed. Harold found that, for the first time, there was a certain sweetness intermingled with the pain that came with remembering his son.

Jackie said nothing, at breakfast. Harold didn't doubt that the anniversary weighed just as heavily on her, but it had been their custom to each cope alone, as if talking about it would force them to double their grief, instead of share their burden. Harold felt that it was time to change that custom.

"It's been five years," he said. And then, "It's hard to *believe* it's been five years."

"I know," Jackie said softly. She was looking at Harold

with an eagerness that suddenly made him wonder whether their mutual silence had always been by mutual consent.

"Do you remember, when Christopher was sick, that one time Doctor Filarski told us that when a cancer patient is in remission, after five years they're considered to have 'rejoined the general population'?" he asked her.

Jackie nodded.

"Well," Harold pushed his plate of uneaten eggs away and continued. "Do you think maybe you and I are ready to 'rejoin the general population'?"

She started to cry then, but it looked like a good kind of crying to Harold, so he did a little of it, himself.

That night, they made buttery popcorn and steaming mugs of hot chocolate, and watched Jimmy Stewart stammer his way through *It's a Wonderful Life* on PBS. It was maudlin, and manipulative, and Harold didn't mind a bit. He was in the right kind of mood.

The next morning, Christmas morning, was a beauty.

Soft snow had been falling for nearly two days, and the grounds of the apartment complex were blanketed in white. Behind the buildings, where people came and went and drove their cars, the snow had been crushed and dirtied—but out front, by the front stoops and the common area, it was pristine.

When Harold walked outside, he looked at the unblemished view before him and knew that it wouldn't have been like that on any other day. On any other day, kids would have been tracking across the common area, making snowballs, and snow forts, and snowmen. On

Christmas morning, however, they were all occupied with more exciting matters.

That was, all except for one.

As Harold scanned the grounds, he discovered, suddenly, that he was not alone. Far across the common area, beside one of the other buildings, there stood Charles Laffin.

The boy was completely still, just standing there with his arms hanging at his sides. He was looking at Harold, and when he saw Harold looking back, he waved. After that he turned and began to walk around to the rear of the building.

"Charles!" Harold shouted. His voice echoed in the frosty quiet of the morning. The only other sound was the distant scraping of a snow shovel.

"Charles! Wait!"

The boy didn't wait. He vanished around the corner.

Harold suddenly was concerned. What kid spent Christmas morning just hanging around, outside?

The same kid who wears a windbreaker when it's freezing out, his mind answered. *The same kid who never plays with other kids. The same kid who's wandering around at 11 o'clock at night, free to talk to the new guy in the building across the way. A neglected kid. Maybe even an abused kid.*

How could he have not realized it, earlier?

"Charles!" Harold called out in his loudest voice, and ran down the front steps. He strode quickly down the sidewalk, and then began to cross the common area, marring the perfect layer of white powder that covered it.

"Charles! I want to talk to you!" Harold started to run

toward the apartment building where he had seen the boy disappear. He was out of shape, and had been smoking far too much, and within a few seconds, his breath was coming out in short, ragged, puffs of vapor. He was still hopeful that he could catch up to Charles, though. And, if he couldn't catch him, he could follow him. A person couldn't move without leaving a pretty clear trail in the freshly fallen snow.

That's what confused Harold the most, when he got to the place where he had seen Charles standing.

There were no prints, no tracks, nothing but the large marks made by Harold's own boots. There was no sign that anyone had been standing there, and no running shoe tracks leading around to the back of the building.

Harold stood there for a while, confused, looking around. Then, on an impulse, he went to the front of the building, climbed the steps, and walked through the doors.

Just like in his own building, there was a bit of an entrance hall, with mailboxes lining the walls. Names, punched out on a labeling gun, identified which box belonged to which tenant.

The labels were testament to the transient nature of apartment dwellers. Some faded letters beneath the labels told Harold that the names had once been painted directly on the metal plates, but that changing them every few months had become a repetitive chore.

Johnson. Lytoff. Shemansky. Harold read them, one by one. There was no Laffin.

Harold was about to leave when he turned to take one last look at the row of names. Something so faded that it was barely there caught his attention. He stepped over to the wall, to take a closer look.

Harold traced the ghost of a line that had once formed the letter "L" in red paint. The letters that had once followed the "L" were obliterated by a label that read *Gaudet*.

Harold worked a thumbnail under the corner of the label. He began to peel. The letters beneath were like pale shadows, but they were readable.

They read *Laffin*.

Harold found himself short of breath again, but not from exertion, and not from the cigarettes. He burst out the front doors of the building and ran down the steps. He didn't stop moving until he had crossed more than half of the common area, plowing a parallel line alongside his first tracks in the virgin snow.

When he did pause to catch his breath, and looked up toward his own living room window, what he saw there hardly even surprised him.

The words, in twinkling lights, simply read *Merry Christmas*. There was no name, in blinking blue, beneath that.

"Did you change it?" he asked Jackie, a few minutes later.

"I didn't change it."

"Do you swear?"

"God! I *swear*, okay? I never touched your lights! Harold, it has *always* just said 'Merry Christmas.' What's wrong with you?"

"I don't know. Nothing. Nothing—I'm sorry," he said. Harold let the matter drop, and averted an argument, and was able to salvage the day.

He and Jackie proceeded to have the best Christmas— the only Christmas—that they had enjoyed in five years.

The winter passed, and spring arrived, and life took on a pleasant rhythm of going to school, and being with Jackie, and even doing a little minor "outside" socializing. Harold had met a fellow named Mark who handled some of the maintenance jobs around the complex, and they had begun to forge a comfortable friendship.

Mark was a stoop-sitter, too. He smoked and drank coffee outside in the winter. When the first hot days came around, he smoked and drank ice-cold beer. Harold joined him in the beverage department, but had cut back on the cigarettes to the point where could almost call himself a non-smoker once more.

Mark had worked there for a decade, mowing lawns, and fixing clogged drains, and replacing the odd pane of broken glass. He was the guy with the label gun, too—a fact that had lodged like a stone in Harold's mind, when he learned of it.

Finally, on a day that was sunny, and warm, and far removed from Christmas, he decided to ask.

"Do you remember a family named 'Laffin' that used to live here?" he asked.

Mark took a swill of beer and nodded.

"Yeah," he said. "A few years back. In that building straight across the way. Why?"

Harold hesitated, but only for a moment.

"Did they have a little boy—about six years old? A little guy named 'Charles'?"

Mark paused for a moment, trying to recall.

"They had two or three kids," he then said. "I didn't know any of their names, but at least one of 'em was a boy. I do remember that, because he was sick with something. You know, he'd get worse, and get better, and then get worse, again. It went like that for a while, and then he died. That was a shame. He was a friendly little kid."

Mark raised the beer can back to his lips, but lowered it as he laughed at a sudden memory.

"That kid—he had all this crazy hair," he said, and waved one hand around his head in an attempt to illustrate his point.

Mark sipped his beer, then, and turned to look at Harold.

"Did you know them?" he asked.

"No," said Harold, and then he told a lie. "We got a piece of mail, once, that was misaddressed to Charles Laffin. It looked like a kid's birthday card."

"Oh," said Mark, accepting the story easily. "Yeah, they moved pretty soon after their kid died. I guess it would be tough to stick around, after something like that. Too many memories. Can you imagine?" He shook his head with genuine sympathy.

"Yeah," said Harold. He could.

He had a little craving then. He came close to asking Mark, "Can I bum a smoke?" But he didn't. Instead, Harold changed the subject—the two men stared out over the greening grass of the common area and talked about power mowers and lawn fertilizer for a while—and then he went back inside.

Later that evening, he lay in bed, holding Jackie, and enjoying the reliable rise and fall of her breath against his chest. He was feeling good, and realized with pleasure that he had been feeling good for quite a long stretch of time. Months, in fact.

But then Harold's wandering mind lit upon the thought of Charles, and the Laffin family, and he braced himself mentally for the expected wave of sadness. It didn't come, however. What arrived, in its place, was a tentative feeling of hope.

Harold knew what the Laffins had gone through. He knew the depth of it. But he also had reason to believe that, wherever they were, they might be enjoying a simple, quiet moment, just as he was now. He had reason to believe that they were perhaps not weighed down by the sadness anymore, that, perhaps, they had found a way to co-exist with it, and not be consumed by it.

According to Mark, it had been a few years. And, given enough time, everyone healed. Some people took longer than others, and sometimes a person needed a little help, but, eventually, everyone rejoined the general population.

That was a good thought. Harold hung on to it until, finally, he drifted into an easy sleep.

Part 2

Reunions

"Though lovers be lost love shall not;

And death shall have no dominion."

—Dylan Thomas, "And death shall have no dominion" (1936)

A Love Story

Long before Nana and Gramps became "Nana and Gramps," they were a young couple in their own right—newly married and in love, breaking the land on their homestead in the middle of the vast Canadian prairie. They had children there, and they forged a life, and they built a home. They lived in that home together until the day that Gramps died.

Their son and daughter were grown by then, out in the world, and each had children of his or her own.

The daughter let a certain amount of time pass after her father's death, and then she spoke to her mother.

"Mom," she said, "do you want to come and live with us now?"

"Oh, no," said Nana. "I could never leave. Your father is still here for me." The daughter took it to mean that his memory was there, in the home her parents had built together, and left it at that.

Sometimes, though, she would overhear her completely coherent mother talking to the walls. Sometimes, she herself felt momentarily wrapped in an invisible source of warmth when she would walk in the door of the old farmhouse.

That's not a bad thing, she thought, and never analyzed it further.

The years passed, and Nana's home remained the hub of the family wheel. Birthdays were celebrated there, with homemade cakes and chicken dinners. Grandchildren visited, sometimes for days at a time, and were returned to their parents once they had been thoroughly spoiled, and stuffed with sweets. Christmases were hosted by Nana as well, with a mouth-watering turkey dinner and a beautiful tree, trimmed with her own handcrafted ornaments.

It was during one such Christmas celebration that Nana's son noticed that the family home was in need of a few repairs.

"It's getting harder for you to keep the place up, Mom," he said to her. "Maybe you should think about moving to an apartment in town."

"I couldn't do that," Nana said, with a smile. "Your father wouldn't know where to find me."

The son was concerned by Nana's answer but decided that it would be best to simply take care of the necessary repairs and let his mother stay where she was both happy and comfortable.

Before he returned to his own life in the city, however, he pulled his own son aside.

"You live close to Nana," he said, "so I want you to look in on her, from time to time. Shovel the driveway in the winter. Mow the lawn in the summer. Take care of things around the house."

The grandson was more than willing to do it. He'd spent many happy times with his Nana, and he loved her very much. It pleased him that he was able to offer something in return for her years of kindness. Often, when he had finished some little chore around the farmhouse, he felt a sense of satisfaction so great, he was able to physically bask in it. It was like a gentle wave that would wash over him and leave him completely at peace.

A few more years passed, and it became apparent to the family that, as well as needing someone to care for the house, Nana needed someone to care for her.

"She would be welcome with us, but she won't leave the house," said the daughter.

"That's true—there's no point in asking," said the son.

After several discussions and a great deal of worrying, a solution was found. The grandson who had been so good at helping Nana was about to be married. He and his wife-to-be would need a home. In the end, they asked Nana if they might stay with her, "until they could get on their feet."

"Of course you can, my dears; it'll be lovely to have the company," said Nana.

Her children sighed with relief.

After the wedding, the young couple moved in. Within days, the wife mentioned to her husband that there was something odd about the farmhouse.

"We aren't the only three here," she said. "I sense, very strongly, that there's someone else."

"Please don't tell me that you want to leave," her husband moaned. "We just got settled."

"Oh, no, it's not like that," said the wife. "There's nothing frightening about it. Whoever is here is very warm, very comforting."

The wife rarely spoke of the presence again, although she felt it often. Occasionally, when she would read the newspaper to Nana, or bring her a steaming cup of tea on a chilly morning, she would sense that she was not alone. Something—some tangible force—would surround her

like a soft blanket and impress upon her a sense of gratitude and appreciation. Once, when she lay down to nap
after several long days of nursing Nana through a bout
with the flu, she felt some unseen person pull the quilt
gently up over her shoulders.

"You're welcome," she mumbled, as she drifted off to
sleep. Later, she would not remember the moment.

The grandson and his wife were happy living with
Nana, in the home where she had raised her children. In
due time, they had children of their own—two little girls,
and then a baby boy, who everyone said had Gramps's
smile. All was well, until one freezing, gray December,
when Nana caught a cold that wouldn't leave her.

The grandson's wife took her to see the doctor.

"This is not good," the doctor said. "If it gets any worse
at all, she will need to be hospitalized."

The young wife drove home, with Nana wheezing in
the passenger seat. She had a drugstore bag filled with pre-
scription medicine in her purse and a good deal of worry
in her heart.

When she turned the pickup truck down the gravel
drive to the house, though, she saw something that lightened her mood.

"Look, Nana!" she said. "It's the Christmas tree!"

Nana's grandson had cut down a magnificent, full
evergreen and was busily evening out its branches so that
it could be brought into the house.

Nana looked at the tree, and smiled. A bit of life came
into her eyes.

"We'll have to make treats for the children tonight,"

she said. "And that box of ornaments is up in the attic, I think. We'll have to bring it down. This is exactly what I need—a tree-trimming party!"

"Are you sure you feel up to it?" the younger woman asked.

"Absolutely. I have always helped to decorate the Christmas tree, and I don't mean to stop now," said Nana.

And so, they made hot apple cider and peanut-butter cookies, and they brought the ornaments down from the attic and decorated the tree. Nana sat in her chair, mostly, directing her grandson to put this bauble here, or that angel there. When it was done, she looked happy, although there was no color in her face.

"Let's all turn in for the night," suggested the grandson's wife. "Tomorrow, we can light the tree and enjoy the full effect."

"Yes, we can admire it tomorrow," Nana said. Then she admitted, "I am very tired tonight."

A few hours later, the grandson's wife woke him.

"Nana's having trouble breathing," she said. "One of us has to take her into town."

"I'll warm up the truck," he said. "You get her ready to go."

The young wife explained to Nana that she needed to go to the hospital. Nana began to cry, which brought on a series of racking coughs.

"I don't want to leave my home," she sobbed.

The young wife was weeping, as well.

"Only for a few days, Nana," she promised. "Only until you get well."

Finally, the frail, elderly woman gave in.

"I'll go," she said. "But bring me my note paper first, and a pen."

The young woman did as she was asked. Nana scrawled some little note to herself, and left it on the bedside table. Then, she permitted her grandson to carry her out into the winter night and seat her in the cab of the truck, next to her little overnight valise.

At the end of the long, gravel driveway, before the truck pulled onto the highway, Nana turned to look at her home. It seemed to her to be a beautiful jewel, laced with glittering frost, set against the black-velvet backdrop of the night sky.

As she was drinking the sight of it in, a bouquet of light and color bloomed in the living room window.

The grandson's wife had plugged in the lights of the Christmas tree.

"Oh," sighed Nana. "She knew I'd look."

But then she forced herself to look away. Nana sat staring forward, gasping for each breath, for the remainder of the trip to the hospital.

The family all gathered, over the two days that followed, as Nana's complexion grew more waxen and her breathing became more labored, and the doctors attached more tubes to her thin, weak body.

Those same doctors shook their heads solemnly, spoke in hushed tones of Nana's advanced age, and made a point of never extending what might have been considered false hope. Nana's children and grandchildren understood what was not being said to them, and they took turns sitting with the elderly woman. There was never a time of the day or night when she was alone.

Late one evening, the grandson with whom Nana lived sat reading, in the stiff chair that was beside her hospital bed. He had been there for several hours, and he longed to stretch his legs and ease his back into a more comfortable position.

Suddenly, he felt himself being cradled, as though in some invisible cushion. For several seconds, his tired muscles felt nothing but soothing warmth and comfort. Then the feeling slipped away from him, and his sense of wonder was broken when his grandmother spoke.

"Oh, Frank," she whispered. Her eyes were open, for the first time in more than a day, and she was smiling. "Is it time to go?" she asked, and then nodded, slightly, as if she had received her answer.

Half an hour later, the grandson stood in front of a payphone in the hospital's lobby. He had a pocketful of change, a long list of phone numbers, and the burden of delivering unhappy, if not exactly unexpected, news.

He had called his own home first, and was surprised when his wife picked up on the first ring.

"Nana's gone, isn't she?" the young woman said.

"How did you know?" her husband asked.

"The house is so empty. I mean, I've been missing Nana these last few days, but this is different. The house is just so *empty*, and I can't get the baby to stop crying. Please come home soon," she said.

He promised that he would.

It was nearly dawn when the grandson walked through the front door, as he had thousands of times before, and was met there by an overwhelming sense of *vacancy*. He knew that he would never mention that conspicuous absence to anyone.

The funeral was held on the Thursday before Christmas. After the service, everyone gathered at the farmhouse to have sandwiches and coffee.

During the gathering, the grandson's wife felt a need to be alone. She found a moment when she was able to slip away from the group, and went upstairs.

She had meant to go to her own bedroom, to spend a few moments resting and gathering her thoughts. Instead, she felt herself drawn to the room that had been Nana's for so many years.

She opened the door and walked in. She had not been in Nana's bedroom since the night that the elderly woman had gone to the hospital, since the night that they had wept together because Nana's heart was broken at the thought of leaving her home.

Everything in the room was as it had been that night. The vaporizer sat on a chair in the corner. The covers on the bed were rumpled. Nana's eyeglasses were folded neatly next to her reading lamp, and the notepaper she had asked for, before leaving, was on the bedside table.

The grandson's wife felt an overpowering sadness then. She wondered what small reminder Nana had left herself, what little detail of life it was that she would never return to take care of. She picked up the note to see.

And she saw that Nana had not been writing to herself at all.

Beneath the pattern of roses and vines that decorated the top of the small sheet of paper, there was a single sentence, written in Nana's weak, uneven scribble.

Frank—I've gone to hospital—love, Evie.

The grandson's wife sat on the edge of the bed for a while, looking at the note. Finally, she set it back on the bedside table.

"I hope you found her, Gramps," she whispered, and then she walked out of the room and returned to her duties as hostess.

Nana's passing took much of the joy out of the holidays for the grandson and his wife, although they went through every celebratory motion for the sake of their children. By Christmas Eve, the girls were flush with excitement and barely able to sleep.

"Santa's coming tonight, isn't he?"

"Will he remember to stop at our house, for sure?"

Eventually, comforted by their parents' repeated assurances that Santa Claus never missed a stop on his appointed rounds, they drifted off. The baby drank a cup of warm milk and settled happily in his crib. The grandson and his wife were then free to make their quiet preparations.

They placed colorfully wrapped gifts beneath the tree, ate most of the cookies that had been left for Santa, and drank half of the cup of cocoa. The grandson used his own boots to make a few mysterious footprints leading from the hearth, and used a tree branch to create reindeer tracks in the snow. Then, satisfied that every detail had been seen to, the couple went to bed.

The younger daughter woke them, only a few hours later.

The stars were still visible in the night sky when the little girl crawled into the warmth of her parents' bed.

"I saw Santa Claus!" she whispered, excitedly.

The grandson smiled, as he tucked the quilt around his daughter. He imagined that she had seen the boot prints and the cookie crumbs, and had let her imagination take flight.

"That's great, honey," he said.

"Yes, but tell us about it later," said his wife, wearily, as she looked at the digital clock on the dresser.

"I will," promised the child. "He had Nana with him, and they were holding hands and looking at the Christmas tree."

The grandson and his wife looked at each other, over their daughter's tousled blonde curls.

"And did Santa and Nana like the tree?" the wife asked, cautiously.

"Oh, yes," said the little girl, in a sleepy voice. "They were smilin'."

An hour later, when her husband and younger daughter were again sleeping soundly, the young wife slipped quietly into her robe and went downstairs.

She wasn't surprised to find the tree festively lit, although she had unplugged it just before retiring for the night.

She did not turn the Christmas lights off but walked past the tree to the broad hallway, where a collection of family photos hung. There were pictures of the children and of her husband and his cousins and of her father-in-law and his sister when they were younger. At the top of them all, like a strong tree from which far-reaching roots had grown, there was a framed black-and-white portrait of Nana and Gramps. It had been taken when they were still Evie and Frank, a young couple with their lives ahead of them. The woman carefully lifted the photo off the hook from which it hung, and carried it with her back to the living room.

She sat on the sofa, and examined the picture. She had never met Gramps, but knew that the dark, curly hair that he had in the picture had turned to white before he died. She knew that he had often worn a beard, and had been a heavy man. It wasn't too difficult to imagine that a four-year-old child might mistake him for Santa Claus, a wandering sort of Santa Claus who had snuck away from Mrs. Claus in order to spend a little time holding hands with Nana.

The woman wiped at her eyes, and smiled at the handsome young couple in the photograph.

"Nana," she said, aloud, "it looks like Gramps got your note."

Suddenly, she was enveloped in the warmth and comfort that she had felt on so many occasions in the farmhouse. But there was something more—a second, equally familiar presence that wound around her, and through her, infusing her with tender affection and a sense of gratitude. The feeling swelled within her for several, glowing seconds, and then slipped away.

Before the radiance left entirely, the young woman spoke.

"It was always my pleasure," she said, as tears spilled down her face. "Always."

And then the feeling was gone, and she found herself alone, watching as the lights strung around the Christmas tree blinked out, one by one. Again, it did not surprise her. She could see the plug at the end of the extension cord resting, not in the outlet, but on the carpet nearby.

The young wife replaced the portrait on the wall, then, and climbed the stairs. As quietly as she had left her bed, earlier, she slipped back into it.

She didn't fall asleep, but lay comfortably, listening to the soft, steady breathing of her husband and daughter. When there was a tinge of pale light in the morning sky, her husband opened his eyes.

"Good morning," she said, softly, to him. "Merry Christmas. I have a story to tell you."

And tell him she did, as the sun rose, and the children all awakened, and the magic of Christmas morning filled the house.

Cookie Randall's Last Rehearsal

Emily had decided that an extra set of arms were at the top of her Christmas wish list.

She had four shopping bags hanging from her left arm, as well as her purse, slung over that shoulder and heavily weighted with life's essentials. She balanced two gift-wrapped boxes in the crook of her right elbow and carried a double non-fat café au lait with her right hand. Her wallet was in her other hand, and her debit card—which she planned to reinsert in her wallet once she found a place in which to set everything down—was temporarily clenched between her front teeth.

Finding a place in which to set everything down appeared to be the challenge, however. The mall was teeming with holiday shoppers, and every one of the tiny, round tables that dotted the area around the coffee kiosk was occupied. Those who sat at them were guarding their highly coveted perches jealously. Emily could see it, in the way that their bags were gathered in close around their feet, defining territorial borders and in the way that they nursed their cappuccinos and mulled cranberry juices, drawing out, as long as possible, their rights as patrons to be seated. It seemed hopeless, and Emily began to wonder if she could manage to simply drop everything she was carrying on the floor around her without destroying the breakable items or spilling her coffee.

"You can sit with me, stranger."

At first, because of the mall noise, the overlapping conversations and the Christmas music blasting from the overhead speakers, Emily wasn't aware that an invitation had been extended to her. She continued to scan the area, clutching her awkward burden.

"Emily! Emily Webb, right? Come sit with me"

Emily stared rather stupidly for a moment at the vaguely familiar woman who was smiling at her from a table only a few feet away. Finally, a mental light came on.

"Bobbi?" she said. With the debit card in her mouth, it came out more like "Wobbi."

"Close enough," the woman laughed. "C'mon, pull up a rock." She patted the extra chair. It was actually more like a hybrid stool and a torture device, being connected rigidly to the table with wrought-iron curlicues, and featuring a seat that, as far as Emily could see, was smaller than absolutely *anyone's* behind. Still, it was a place to rest. An oasis of relief. So Emily put her coffee on the table, set down her packages and sank gratefully into the seat that was opposite her old friend, Roberta Curtis.

"Emily, it has been a long time," said Bobbi.

"Too long," Emily agreed. It had been more than a decade since she had seen Bobbi, and more than two since they had been close. Bobbi Curtis had been Emily Webb's best friend in the whole world, in the years before adolescence and the adolescent behavior that eventually peeled them apart.

"So, how are you, Bobbi?" Emily asked, although she could see the answer plainly enough. Bobbi looked fit and was well-dressed and had her hair expertly cut and subtly streaked to hide any gray that might have had the audacity to show itself. In comparison, Emily felt like some sweaty pack animal, and she vowed to never again leave the house without looking good enough to run into someone from her past.

All of that ran through Emily's mind in the time that it took Bobbi to say, "I'm fine," and then ask Emily about herself.

"Oh, fine, generally," Emily said. She struggled to find some way to explain her life in 25 words or less, without sounding too pathetic or defensive. "Still married to Fred, you know," she finally said. "We have a couple of kids now. I'll probably go back to work once they're a bit older." She shrugged.

Yeah, that sums up 15 years nicely, she thought.

But if Bobbi Curtis thought that Emily had provided an inadequate explanation for the span of time involved, she did not let on. She asked the children's names, and their ages, and made Emily produce the photographs that she knew were certain to be in her purse. She was interested, and complimentary, and, soon, the two women were sharing stories, laughing and traveling in what Emily often thought of as "the way-back machine." It was time-travel, powered by reminiscence.

Emily reminded Bobbi of the times when they had copied one another's homework, with spelling mistakes carelessly left intact. ("And we'd be absolutely *bewildered* when we got caught!")

Bobbi had Emily howling over the time they had pooled their money to buy a tube of discount-bin bright blue creme eyeshadow, and had ended up with identical patches of eczema. ("Did yours ooze? *Mine* oozed!")

The women shared stories, laughter and gossip, until both felt that it was time to address what was an inevitable subject.

"Remember Cookie Randall?"

The question was rhetorical. There was no way that either of them could have forgotten Cookie Randall, or the thing that had happened to her.

When they had both been 12, and still the best of friends, Emily and Bobbi had been members of the Whispering Hills Junior High All-Girls Choir. Cookie Randall, their small-town school's music teacher, had been the choir mistress.

They had to call her "Miss Randall" to her face, of course, as a show of respect. Behind her back, however, Emily, Bobbi, and all the other girls found that they could not refrain from referring to Cookie by her given name, once they had discovered what a ridiculous moniker it was.

"*Cookie's* wearing perfume, today," someone would say.

"That's because *Cookie's* got the hots for Mr. Kowalski," someone else would add.

"Nah. *Mr. Lionel* is more *Cookie's* type," some pre-adolescent wit would chime in, and everyone would erupt in a fit of giggles, because Mr. Lionel still had raging acne at the age of 30, and carried his lunch in a briefcase.

Naturally, Cookie Randall was a "type" all her own. She was plain, and awkward, with lanky black hair that was chopped off just below her ears, and she had thick, wire-rimmed glasses that did not quite hide the fact that her two eyes tended to gaze in just slightly different directions. Cookie didn't know how to dress, and, so, had adopted a uniform of sorts—a plain, white blouse, and shapeless, below-the-knee skirt, topped with a crocheted sweater vest in either navy or tan. Her shoes, in an era of strappy disco sandals, were chunky and solid, and her thick, beige panty-hose always seemed to collect in folds around her ankles. She lived alone in a little, rented farmhouse, and drove a yellow hatchback. She was unmarried. *Chronically* unmarried.

The truth was that if Cookie Randall had a passion in her life, it was not for Mr. Kowalski or Mr. Lionel or any other man, but for the choir. Cookie loved her All-Girls Choir, and it showed, because she was good at directing it.

She made the girls audition to join, so that being a member *meant* something. She challenged them with difficult pieces, and then rewarded them for rising to meet that challenge by slipping in a few fun, popular arrangements. Most of all, she managed to inspire them into performances that they had not known they were capable of. Her enthusiasm tended to be infectious, and after spending a few months in Cookie's choir, a girl usually loved it as much as Cookie did.

Aside from the annual festival competition, and a song sung here or there for a special occasion (the girls performed a jazzy rendition of *Happy Birthday* when the school's librarian turned 65), there were two major concerts they had to prepare for every year. There was the annual "Spring Fling," and then, of course, there was the Christmas pageant.

The Christmas pageant was clearly Cookie's favorite.

She would be selecting the program during the still-warm days of September and would have the girls in rehearsal for it before Halloween. Every year, Cookie followed the same blueprint. There would be two Christmas carols—one religious, one secular. There would be something with a bit of bop to it; a crowd-pleaser like "Jingle Bell Rock" or "Santa Bring My Baby Back." And then there would be the crown jewel of the evening, some carefully chosen, excruciatingly difficult classical piece.

For the Christmas pageant of 1977, the classical piece was "Ave Maria," and Emily was the soloist. It was the last year that Cookie Randall directed the choir. It was the only year that Emily joined. The year before, she had been too young, and the year after, even thinking about it made her sad.

By the end of that November, Cookie had her girls rehearsing three times every week—Wednesdays during the lunch hour, and Monday and Thursday evenings. It was the rehearsal held on the first Thursday night of that December that everyone talked about for years. Even after decades had passed, Emily thought of it often and even dreamed about it on occasion.

The weather had been mild that evening, and most of the girls had walked back to school after having their dinners. There were 15 of them who gathered in the aging auditorium. For once, by some rare coincidence, every one of them was on time. What was even more rare was that Cookie Randall was not.

For a few minutes, the girls had lolled about on the carpeted risers, enjoying the gift of time in which they could do nothing but gossip and relax. Then, someone recognized that they had been given an even greater gift—

the opportunity to complain indignantly about a teacher's tardiness—and the girls jumped upon that.

"I can't believe this. I have a test to study for," someone complained.

"She's *obviously* not going to show up—let's go to the Burger Bar," someone else suggested.

"Who wants to go for a smoke?" asked one 13-year-old sophisticate, who had three menthol cigarettes stolen from her mother's handbag secreted away in her own beaded, fringed, leather purse.

Emily and Bobbi, the two youngest girls there, had been sitting together, a bit apart from the group.

"What do you think?" Emily had asked, quietly. "How long should we wait?"

Bobbi looked at the clock and shrugged. She was busy fiddling with a tube of pineapple-flavored lip gloss.

"Maybe five more minutes?" she suggested, and applied the third coat of gloss that she had put on since the girls had arrived.

But just then, before the bitchy girls could leave in a huff, or the tough girls could go smoke, or Bobbi could slick on more fruity lip balm, Cookie Randall showed up. She burst through the double doors in a sudden flurry of sheet music and stale perfume. Her hip-length vest—the navy one, that particular day—was hanging askew on her bony frame, and loops of yarn had been snagged loose in a couple of places. The shoulder strap of Cookie's bulging bag had slipped to the crook of her elbow, and the bag itself bumped along behind her, bouncing off her left calf with every second step that she took.

"I'm sorry, girls. I'm sorry to be late," she mumbled. "I, ah... I, um," Cookie tapped the side of her eyeglasses, as explained, "I broke my—my glasses."

As if they couldn't see. Cookie had obviously snapped the bridge of her spectacles, and then mended it, as best she could, with a wad of silvery duct tape. The bulging tape cast made the frames teeter from side to side on her thin nose, and the overall effect was that she looked more cockeyed than ever. When she scanned the room, in her distracted way, with her eyes seeming to aim in every direction at once, there was more than one indiscreet snicker.

"So we're all here, then?" she said, as she dropped everything she had been carrying in one messy pile beside the piano. "Good. Good. We have a lot of work to do tonight."

Cookie waved the girls over, and they formed a horse-shoe-shaped line behind the piano bench. Altos stood on the left; sopranos fell in to the right.

"I can't stay late, just because we're starting late," one girl griped. It was a ninth-grade queen named Kari, who wore huge hoop earrings and plucked her eyebrows into severe arches.

"Yeah," agreed one of Kari's minions, "we have other things to do."

Cookie, who was normally not confrontational, turned on them.

"If you don't want to be here, leave now," she said. "If you're not ready to work, leave now. If you can't stay until we're finished, tonight, *leave now*. But understand that you will not be receiving your extra credit, and you will not be returning to my choir!"

Emily and Bobbi looked at each other in discreet exaltation. There was nothing quite as sweet as being present when the older girls—who held power over them, and liked to abuse it—got a dressing down.

"Have I made myself clear?" Cookie Randall said then, and scanned the entire row of girls, searching for any dissension that needed to be dealt with.

A dozen voices mumbled, "Yes, Miss Randall."

Kari and her friends shrugged, in their defiant way.

"I guess," said one of them, in a sulky tone, and the matter was settled.

"Scales, then," said Cookie, and she struck a chord on the piano.

Usually, the girls practiced their scales for five minutes. Sometimes, there would be some other vocal exercise added to the warm-up time. On that night, however, Cookie forced the girls to sing their scales as a group, and then individually, for more than 20 minutes.

"This note! *This* note," she would snap, impatiently, as she hammered on a piano key.

Bobbi felt that they were all being unfairly painted with the same brush.

"*We* weren't mouthing off," she complained to Emily at one point. The comment was too hushed to reach Cookie Randall's ears, but was not lost on Kari and her devotees. The minute it was said, one of them turned to whisper to the other two. Suddenly, three pairs of heavily made-up eyes were glaring at Bobbi, who rarely concerned herself with such public opinion, and Emily, who cared deeply about it. Emily felt her face growing warm, in response, and she tried to hide behind her sheaf of mimeographed music sheets.

An hour later, Cookie still seemed out of sorts. She was pushing the girls relentlessly, demanding that they work on each piece twice as long as they did normally.

Nothing was being allowed to slide. The difficult harmonies were repeated until she was satisfied that they had been perfectly accomplished, and every sour note was punished with an additional set of scales. As the hour grew later, the girls sang off key more frequently, and Cookie's frustration grew.

"Miss Randall, we have two more weeks to practice," said a pimply ninth-grade alto who rarely spoke. "We'll get it right, by then."

Cookie pinched the tape on her glasses, trying in vain to make them sit properly on her face.

"No, Andrea," she said, "I fear you won't. We've been practicing for six weeks. If you girls can't get this right tonight, you never will. Now, let's run through 'Ave Maria.'"

Cookie played the first four bars, then broke off, abruptly.

"Where do you think you're going?"

Emily looked up from her sheet music. Kari Kessler was standing at the double doors, poised to push them open.

"I need a drink of water," she explained, in a less-than-respectful tone.

"Later." Cookie spoke briskly. "Right now, we're working on 'Ave Maria.'"

"So, go ahead," said Kari. "I'll be back in a minute.

What does it matter if I'm not here, anyway? It's not like I'm doing the solo."

She shot a black look at Emily, then. Emily lowered her eyes and felt the flush creeping back into her cheeks. Two months earlier, she had auditioned against Kari for the privilege of singing the difficult solo. Emily had won that battle, but, as the weeks passed, it had begun to seem less and less like a strategically sound move in the over-all war.

"Get back in your place, or don't come back," Cookie said to Kari. She sounded serious.

Kari spent a moment weighing her options. Eventually, she decided to saunter—very slowly—back to her place in line with the other sopranos.

Cookie began to play once more, and the girls began to sing.

The choir sang en masse for the first part, and then there was a brief piano interlude. Following that was Emily's solo. At least, it would have followed, had she not missed her cue.

"I'm sorry," she stammered, when the music stopped and everyone looked at her.

"Pay attention, please," said Cookie. Her voice was sharp, but the reprimand could have been much worse, given her mood. Emily considered herself to have gotten off lucky.

Cookie turned back to the keyboard, and played the musical passage once more. Emily was so anxious to not miss her cue that she stepped on it, instead. It was enough to distract her through the entire solo. She hit two flats that should have been sharp, and her voice cracked on a high note. She forgot to breathe at another point, and ended up gasping for air in the middle of a note that she should have been sustaining. One of the older girls laughed aloud; quickly disguising it as a fit of coughing. Emily wished for nothing more than to crawl away and hide.

Cookie Randall was not about to allow such indulgences.

"Let's all do it again," she said, briskly. "This needs some work."

So, they did it again. And again. And again.

"Franz Schubert is *spinning* in his grave!" Cookie shrieked, at one point. "*Spinning!* We will do this *again!*"

It was a relentless and, seemingly hopeless, pursuit of perfection. And for every time Cookie had the choir go through the entire piece, she had Emily perform her solo twice.

"It's breathy," she complained, after one attempt. "Use your diaphragm. Use your...Here, here..." Cookie leapt off the piano bench and patted Emily's abdomen with her cold, rawboned hand.

"Sing from *here*, Emily," she said. "This is where it comes from. This is where you get *passion*."

One of the altos snickered. Emily wanted to die.

"Is there a problem, over there?" asked Cookie.

Silence.

"I *said*, is there a problem?"

There was a long pause then, but, finally, someone stepped up to meet the challenge.

"The *problem* is that you've got a first-year doing a solo, and she's never going to get it right. We're all sick of this, and we should have gone home half an hour ago."

It was Kari Kessler. She flipped her bleached hair over her shoulder for full effect, and stood, arms crossed, prepared to stare Cookie Randall down.

Except Cookie Randall wasn't in the mood to be stared down.

"Half an hour ago?" she hissed. "I don't think so. Nor do I think you'll be going home half an hour from *now*, unless you all manage to perform so beautifully that I feel you've been touched by the very hand of God!"

A look of exasperation settled over Cookie's features then, and she looked from one girl to the next, as if searching desperately for someone who might understand her.

"The pageant is in two weeks," she said. "Two weeks! You can't put this off, anymore. You have to *do the work!* You have to *concentrate!* We are out of time, truly, and if you can't master this tonight, you will never have another chance to do it."

Cookie drew herself up to her full, gangly height, then, and made an announcement.

"We will not leave here tonight, until you girls can sing 'Ave Maria' with *passion*."

And that was the moment when Kari Kessler, who seemed to believe that one might as well be hanged for a sheep as a lamb, asked the question:

"What could you possibly know about 'passion' ...*Cookie?*"

Later, Emily couldn't say what made her do it. It might have been the humiliation that she saw in Cookie's wonky eyes. It might have been outrage over the brazen *indiscretion* of saying aloud the things that most of them meant harmlessly enough, when they giggled and whispered behind a teacher's back. It might have been than she was sick to death of Kari Kessler's big mouth. Or she might have simply been overtired. But, for whichever reason, she stood up to Kari, and stood up *for* Cookie.

"You shut *up*, Kari!" Emily screamed. The words were out of her mouth before she had a chance to edit them, and then there was nothing to do but follow through.

"We're sick of you! Everybody's working hard tonight, and it would be easier if you weren't always opening your dumb mouth! And Miss Randall's working hard, too. And that's what you call her—*Miss Randall!* Stop being so juvenile!"

The auditorium fell silent. Emily felt something like static electricity, tingling beneath her scalp, and she knew that bright red blotches were forming a patchwork on her skin, from her chest to her forehead. For once, she wasn't embarrassed. For once, she didn't care. She turned to Cookie Randall, who had dropped her teacher's mask of detachment, and was showing some combination of admiration and gratitude.

"I'm ready to sing again," Emily said.

Cookie nodded, and returned to the piano. She placed her hands gently on the keys, and began to play the sweet melody that led into the solo.

And then, perfectly on key, perfectly in time, with power, and control, and *passion*, Emily sang.

She sang her solo piece, and then the other girls joined in. Fifteen voices blended together, with sweetness, and harmony, and strength. The auditorium filled with the haunting strains of "Ave Maria," a performance of "Ave Maria" that absolutely soared.

When it was finished, and the last note had faded away, there was silence. The girls—even the nasty ninth-grade girls—stared at one another through eyes wide with amazement. They had been shocked by the vision of their own potential.

Slowly, Cookie Randall turned to face them.

"That was magnificent," she said, simply. "Sing it exactly that way, at the pageant. You may go."

The shuffling sounds of movement began. There were a few coughs, and the fabric whispers of coats being shrugged on, and the muffled rattling of compacts and key chains and loose change, as purses were collected.

The girls filed out of the auditorium in twos and threes, and the echoing sounds of their footsteps could be heard down the school's long, deserted hallway.

Emily held back, a little. She zipped her down-filled jacket slowly, and took a long time rearranging her sheet music in its binder.

Bobbi was growing impatient.

"Come *on*," she whispered excitedly, as she leaned against one of the doors to hold it open. "Let's go! I have to tell you what Kari just said to Shelley!"

Emily nodded, but held up one hand asking Bobbi to wait. She couldn't go, just yet. She couldn't leave without first talking to Cookie.

Not that Cookie was looking talkative. She looked tired, despondent and broken. She was still sitting on the piano bench, but her shoulders were slumped forward and her big, homely hands were resting in her lap. She was holding her glasses, there, and half-heartedly examining the tape with which she had mended them.

"Miss Randall?" Emily's voice was small, and Cookie Randall seemed to be so far away. There was no reaction.

"Miss Randall?" Emily spoke with more force; from her *diaphragm*, and Cookie slowly raised her head.

"Emily?" she said.

And then Emily realized she had prepared nothing to say. She didn't even know what she wanted to express, exactly.

You're a good teacher, she was thinking; *a special teacher, even. Sometimes you make us laugh, but most of us would never want to hurt your feelings.*

Thank you, Miss Randall, was what she was feeling, but she didn't know how to say it. In the end, she simply asked Cookie a meaningless question.

"How did you break your glasses?"

"Oh," said Cookie, and she looked back down at the twisted wire frames in her hands. She let out a small, soft laugh, and then she turned to answer Emily.

"I just had a little accident," was all she said.

The next day, everyone at school learned that, on the way home from rehearsal, Cookie Randall had had a *big* accident. Her yellow hatchback hit a patch of black ice and left the road, just as she had been approaching the bridge on the way out of town. The car tumbled over the guard rail, and down the embankment to the river. Cookie might have been alright, had she not hit her face on the steering wheel and blacked out. But, because of that, she didn't know that the nose of her car had broken through the thin layer of ice at the river's edge, and she didn't know that the little car had slid just a few feet below the water. She didn't know, because

she was unconscious, and a few minutes after the frigid black water filled her lungs, she was dead.

Bobbi's father, who was the town cop given the unsavory duty of fishing Cookie Randall out of the river, later told Bobbi and Emily that if Cookie had been able to simply lift her head, she wouldn't have drowned.

"The back of her hair wasn't even wet," he said.

Two weeks later, the Whispering Hills Junior High All-Girls Choir performed poignantly, in Cookie Randall's memory, at the annual Christmas pageant.

All Emily had been able to think about were the broken glasses, and the back of poor Cookie's head.

The mall was still swarming with frazzled holiday shoppers. Christmas music still blared from the overhead speakers. There were still the flashing lights, and glitzy decorations, and sales signs as far as the eye could see. But none of it penetrated the circle of reverie which Emily and Bobbi had drawn around their cramped little table.

"I still think about that night, all the time," said Emily. Her hands cradled the coffee cup that had been empty for more than half an hour.

"I know," said Bobbi. "It was, bar none, the strangest experience of my life." She shook her head, solemnly, and chewed on the end of her neon-yellow stir stick.

Emily was reminded of the pineapple lip gloss, and smiled.

"Do you think she knew?" She asked the question of Bobbi, then answered it, herself. "I do. I don't think that she did it on purpose—you know, committed suicide—

but I do think that she *somehow* knew, on *some* level, that she was about to die. I think she knew that it was her last chance to whip us into shape for that pageant."

Emily looked at Bobbi then, expecting her to offer an opinion. But Bobbi was saying nothing. Bobbi was wearing an odd expression, and had dropped the plastic stir stick.

"Well, what do you think, Bobbi?"

"I think...Emily...There's something that I thought you would have figured out, by now."

"What?"

There was a pause, and Emily had to repeat herself.

"Bobbi—*what?*"

Bobbi took a deep breath.

"Cookie Randall lived out south of town, right? But they found her on the south bank of the river. Didn't you ever wonder about that?"

Emily shrugged.

"No. I guess...No."

Bobbi raised her eyebrows emphatically.

"Well I did. And I kept asking my dad about it, until, finally, years later, he admitted that they just told us all what they thought was *easiest* for us to cope with— because we were just kids, you know?"

Emily shook her head slowly.

"No, I *don't* know," she said. "What are you trying to tell me, Bobbi?"

Bobbi leaned in close.

"Cookie Randall didn't die on the way home from rehearsal," she said. "Cookie Randall died on the way *to* rehearsal. She never made it there, Emily."

Suddenly, all Emily could think about was the ice-cold

feeling of Cookie's big, angular hand pressing against her flat, 12-year-old stomach.

"She never made it there," she said, flatly.

Bobbi nodded.

"I would have told you, but by the time I found out, we had sort of gone our separate ways. And later, you know...Well, I just thought you would have eventually figured it out."

"I never did," said Emily. "I never, *ever*...Oh my *God!*"

"Yeah," said Bobbi, and she nodded. "That's kind of how I felt, too."

The women said their goodbyes eventually, trading addresses and phone numbers before going their separate ways. Each promised to call the other. Both knew that they would likely not meet again until their next chance encounter.

Emily packed her many purchases into her van, and then returned to the mall to make one more. When she was unwrapping it, that evening, after the kids were in bed, her husband peered over her shoulder.

"Classical," he said. "That's a change of pace, for you."

Emily nodded.

"I used to love this," she said, as she ran her finger over the front of the CD jewel case. "I'd sort of forgotten."

She got the portable CD player, then, and went into the bedroom. She lay on the bed, with the lights turned down, and found the track she wanted.

Emily closed her eyes, and pushed the play button. For the first time in years, she listened to the sailing voice of a soprano singing "Ave Maria."

The melody wound its way through her, dipping, and soaring, and building to inspirational heights. When the final strains of music died away, she took the headphones off, and smiled.

"Thank you, Miss Randall," she said, and this time, she said it aloud.

Then she put the compact disc away in her dresser, where it would wait safely until the next time that Cookie came back.

The Christmas Caller

It was close to Christmas Day, and the preparations had been made.

The large freezer had been stocked with mincemeat tarts and shortbread and sugar cookies cut in clever little seasonal shapes and dusted with red and green candy sprinkles. Gifts that had been carefully chosen over the weeks and months previous had been wrapped in festive papers, artistically topped with ribbons and bows, and placed at the foot of the tree. The tree itself was a magnificent creation—festooned with a shimmering garland and resplendent with the twinkling red lights and shiny gold balls that looked so good together. And there were other decorative touches, as well—the Christmas needlepoint cushions on the sofa, the little porcelain pieces of the Christmas village set out upon the mantle, the Christmas china waiting in the cabinet, and the welcoming Christmas wreath that hung upon the front door.

It had all been prepared, and it was all for nothing. The woman who had worked so hard sat at her kitchen table, with a cold, forgotten, cup of coffee before her and a letter in her hands. The letter told her that her only child, her son, would not be able to make it home for the holidays.

The young man lived in Chicago. The family home was in Texas. The miles in between meant that mother and son did not see each other often. The woman had been eagerly anticipating the rare holiday visit, and her disappointment over its cancellation was crushing.

After a very long time, she finally rose from the table, poured her coffee down the sink, and put the letter away in a cubbyhole of the antique desk that occupied one corner of the living room. At least her husband would be pleased, she thought, and the thought was laced with bitterness.

"I'm not surprised. That boy never could keep his word."

The woman's husband was working on his third pork chop, mopping up gravy with a piece of floury biscuit. He was pretending to be upset, but the woman, whose own dinner sat nearly untouched in front of her, knew that he was reveling in the news.

"Don't you go sending those presents to him," the man said. "If he can't get here, he doesn't need 'em. You've got receipts, right? They can be returned?"

The woman said mildly that she didn't know; she'd have to check. Inside, she seethed at the cruelty of the suggestion.

Her husband was not the father of her son. He was his stepfather, and, although he had lived with the boy for years, no bond had grown between them. Instead, where affection might have taken root, hostility and mis-understanding had flourished. The tension had become greater each year. By the time the boy was 16, he felt he could no longer stay.

"If I go, things will be better," he had said. "And I'll visit, all the time."

All the time ended up being some of the time, when it became apparent that living apart had done nothing to

"But, you *know* who's there," the woman pleaded. "He's the only one who rings the bell that way!" She had her feet pushed into slippers and her housecoat wrapped around her, already.

"I said 'stay,'" said the husband, and he shrugged into his own flannel robe as he walked out of the room.

The woman sat nervously on the edge of the bed and waited for the sound of rising voices. Her husband was angry at having been wakened. Her son would be angry at having driven such a long way only to be greeted with hostility.

"Please don't fight," she whispered. "Please, please, please don't fight." She was so happy that her son had changed his mind and come home, and she didn't want his arrival marred by an argument.

There was no argument, though. There was no joyous reunion, either. Within minutes, the woman's husband returned to the bedroom.

"Nobody there," he told her, as he crawled back under the covers.

"What do you mean?" she demanded. He was lying to her, and she knew it.

"I mean, there was nobody there!" he bellowed. "Now, get back in bed and let's get some sleep!"

The woman stepped out of her slippers and draped her housecoat over the foot of the bed. She slipped back between the sheets, keeping quite deliberately to her side of the mattress. As she lay there, body rigid and eyes wide, she smoldered over the injustice of her husband's actions.

My son came all this way, she thought. *He drove through the night. And he was turned away from his own door. And in the rain, too.*

ease the young fellow's strained relationship with his step-father. Then some of the time became hardly ever after the boy moved north.

The woman always hoped for his return; for the sound of his quick, light step on the wooden porch, and the staccato ringing of the doorbell that announced his presence. Instead, there were phone calls, and letters, and cards on Mother's Day and her birthday. But she had not seen her son in more than a year, and the canceled Christmas visit meant she would have to wait longer still.

After supper, the leftovers went into the refrigerator, and the dishes were washed. The woman tried to read a magazine while her husband watched television, but found that she could not concentrate.

"I'm going to bed," she announced finally, and left the room.

An hour later, when her husband joined her, she feigned sleep.

Some time later, she truly was sleeping when the sound of the doorbell awakened her. Even before she opened her eyes, a smile was spreading on her lips.

Ring-ding-a-ding-ding-a-ding. It was her son's signature announcement.

It was also 1:30 in the morning, and the woman's husband was furious.

"You stay right here!" he ordered, when the woman leapt out of bed to go answer the door. "It's the middle of the damn night; we're not going to just throw the door open to whoever's there."

There had been a steady drizzle all of the previous evening, which had turned into a downpour. Cold rain soaked the streets and beat down on the roof of the house. The woman lay awake in bed for the rest of the night, listening to the storm and watching the wriggling shadows cast on the bedroom curtains as the streetlights shone through rivulets of water on the window.

The next morning was silent. The man and woman sat across from one another in the breakfast nook, nursing their own resentments. He consumed three eggs and a plateful of bacon and hash browns, because he tended to eat when he was angry. She stirred a great deal of cream and sugar into her coffee, and then let it go cold. Neither one spoke, and, eventually, the man put on his jacket, picked up his briefcase, and left by the back door to go to work. The woman made herself busy at the front of the house as he left, so she would not have to kiss him goodbye.

The rain had moved on. Through the picture window in the living room, the woman looked out at the puddles that dotted the street and the high haze of cloud that was moving to the west.

The porch will be a mess, with all the mud, she thought. The steps and landing of the covered front entrance had just been painted, and the woman liked to keep them spotless. She had washed them the previous afternoon, just after the postman had delivered her son's letter. With the rain, and the mud, she knew that she would have to wash them again, as soon as someone walked up to the front door.

The thought made her pause.

Her husband had said there had been no one at the door. But the bell had sounded clearly. Anyone who rang the bell would have had to walk up the steps, and across the broad wooden landing. It had been raining for all of the previous evening, so they would have left tracks. The woman thought about this for a moment, and then went to the front door and opened it.

The landing was clean. But that did little to change her mind. If anything, it increased the degree of resentment that she had been feeling.

It only means that he took a minute to wipe the steps, after sending my child away, she thought, and she could feel the grudge settling into her stomach like a leaden weight.

Things had to change, that much was clear. She had to start standing up for herself, and her son. She had suffered the last insult, the last offense...

The telephone interrupted her internal rant.

She ran to answer it, hopeful that it was her boy, calling from a motel, or the house of a friend. She would tell him to come right over. She would tell him that if he was not welcome, then neither was she. She would tell him that they were going to have the finest Christmas they had ever celebrated, together.

"Hello?"

"Yes, Mrs..."

The disappointment was immediate. It was a male voice, on the other end of the line, but it was not her son. It was a stranger.

When the stranger identified himself as a police officer, from Dallas, the disappointment turned to cold fear.

The woman learned that her son had decided to come

home for the holidays, after all. And he *had* been driving through the dark night and the pouring rain. Then she learned that there had been a terrible accident. She went numb as the stranger's distant voice asked if she would be able to travel to Dallas to identify the body.

"I will," she said, simply, and began to hang up the phone.

Then, it occurred to her to ask a single question.

"Wait!" she said. "What time did he...What time did it happen?"

There was a pause, as the police officer consulted the accident report.

"About 1:30 this morning, ma'am," he finally said.

It was the same time that the doorbell had sounded out the young man's signature ring.

When the woman's husband arrived home from work, he found her wearing her best suit, sitting patiently on the sofa, with her handbag in her lap. A packed suitcase sat by the front door.

"I have a taxi coming," she said, and then she explained the rest.

"I'm very sorry," he said, and he did appear to be shaken.

"I'm sorry, too," the woman spoke, softly. Then she looked at her husband and sighed.

"I don't blame you anymore for last night, obviously," she explained, "but I do blame us both for all the other times. You for being cruel, and me, for being weak."

The taxi arrived, then, and the woman stood up and gathered her things.

"I'll be gone for a few days," she said.

"But why?" Her husband was bewildered. "It's only a day trip," he said.

"I know," she nodded, "but it's very important to me—I want to spend one last Christmas near my son."

The woman walked out the door to the waiting taxi. The man stood in front of the living room window, and watched her go. He raised his hand slightly to wave, but she never turned back to look, so there was no point.

By the time he was eating his cold dinner, from a TV tray in the living room, she was already in a different taxi-cab, in Dallas.

The cab driver was a friendly, chatty sort who asked the woman what her plans for Christmas were.

"I am spending it with family," she said, and then turned to look out the window.

The driver, who could sense when a passenger didn't want to talk, left her alone with her thoughts.

Christmas with the family, he mused, silently.

He supposed that wasn't always a good thing.

The Road Trip

The smell of burning plastic filled the air.

"Get the elf! Get the elf!" someone screamed, and suddenly, one of Santa's helpers was tumbling across the floor, showing its grotesquely molten face with every turn.

There was a whoosh of flame, and the cinders of what had been a glittering, tinsel rope began to float down to the floor.

Some terrified person attempting to flee the disturbing scene tripped, and fell on top of a reindeer. There was a sickening crunch, as one of its legs snapped off.

Then a horrified child began to shriek, "Santa Claus! Santa Claus!" and Lloyd turned, knowing exactly what he would see.

He knew, because it all was unfolding just as it had in his dream, on so many occasions, so many miles away.

Lloyd Bricker Jr. had begun to have the terrible dream in the weeks leading up to Christmas. It was always the same for him: chaos, and flaming destruction, and, at the center of it all, the hauntingly familiar man in the Santa Claus suit. Santa was calling him, in the dream; calling out to Lloyd, because he needed his help. Lloyd would try to help. He would walk toward the man, in that slow, underwater motion of dreamscapes, and tear away the stranger's flowing, false beard. Beneath the beard, he would see the evidence of 30 years' worth of hard living and hard drinking. And beneath that, he would see the recognizable face. It was the same one that smiled out at him from the worn, yellowing photo that he carried in a little plastic sleeve in his snakeskin wallet.

"It was my very own father," Lloyd told his platinum-haired wife, Betty, on the morning after one particularly bad night. Just after midnight, he had awakened, scream-ing and in a cold sweat. It had taken hours before the gentle motion of the waterbed was able to lull him back to sleep.

"What an awful nightmare," Betty soothed. She shook her head, clucked her tongue and dropped a plateful of sausages on the tablecloth.

"Well, here's the thing," said Lloyd, and he paused, to slick back the sides of his black pompadour. "I'm not so sure it's just a nightmare. I'm beginning to think that it's more like a psychic hotline thing, you know: a premoni-tion. I believe that my daddy might be calling out to me."

"Oh, but honey," said Betty, who stood at the stove fry-ing eggs, "you know your daddy died a long time ago."

Lloyd chewed thoughtfully on a link of sausage.

"Well, now, I'm not entirely certain of that," he said. "Just lately, I'm a little blurry on whether Momma used to say he *was* dead, or that she *wished* he was dead. He did lose some favor with her, leaving so unceremoniously, as he did, just prior to my own birth."

"It's true," Betty nodded ruefully.

"But this, I think, is a message," said Lloyd. "I think my Daddy is out there, somewhere, and in need of my assistance."

Betty brought the eggs to the table, and slid three of them from the serving dish to Lloyd's plate.

"Are you sure it's not just the season?" she asked. "You know how you long for family ties, when they start to show those emotional commercials, with all the snow, and everything, on the TV."

"I admit that I am a sucker for the magic of Christmas," said Lloyd, "but this is different. This is like those programs about psychic miracles. You know, the ones hosted by that fella with all the wavy hair who used to do the news. Ketchup?"

Betty set the bottle down in front of him.

"You are sensitive to such things," she admitted. "I'll never forget the time you predicted that you were going to lose your job, and then it happened!"

"Three times, it happened!" said Lloyd, as he shoved a forkful of mangled eggs into his mouth.

"You have a gift," said Betty, and sat down to eat her own breakfast.

"It's true," said Lloyd, "but it's a gift with a dark side, to be sure."

That night, Lloyd was lulled to sleep by the peaceful, distant sound of howling coyotes. He awoke to the deafening hammer of his own heartbeat, and the suffocating certainty that the trailer's wood-paneled walls were closing in on him.

He had suffered the nightmare again. There had been something different about it, though—a sense of increasing urgency. Also, amid the flames, and horror, and destruction, above the screams, and sounds of stampeding feet, Lloyd had heard the man in the Santa suit speak to him.

In a slow, echoing dream voice, he had spoken, and his lips appeared out of sync with his voice.

"*What's keepin' you, boy?*" he had said.

As soon as the tide of panic within Lloyd began to recede a little, he shook Betty's shoulder.

"Baby, wake up," he said.

"Lloyd Jr.?" she asked, in a confused, sleepy voice. "Did you lose your hairnet, again?"

"Betty," Lloyd said, "how much cash money do we have?"

Betty sat up and propped herself against the black velvet headboard of the waterbed.

"Well," she said, as she rubbed her eyes. "There's 30 dollars hid under the canned lunch meat that we were saving for a turkey dinner and a little Christmas tree. Oh! And we haven't paid the rent money to Buster Farley yet, so *technically* we've got..."

"We got enough," Lloyd said, and leapt out of bed.

"Pack the Shark," he ordered, as he wriggled into a pair of skintight black jeans. "We're goin' on a road trip."

The Shark was a powder-pink '59 Cadillac Coupe that had been so nicknamed because of its enormous fins. While the moon still hung high in the starry night sky, Lloyd and Betty loaded it with all of the things that would be necessary for their journey.

There was a worn, canvas suitcase that held changes of clothing, and a good supply of hair gel. There was a cooler, filled with soda pop and a can of spray cheese. There were saltines, upon which to spray the cheese, and a package of licorice whips. And, in a brown paper shopping bag, on the fuzzy leopard-print covered back seat, were a few small packages wrapped in fancy paper. They were Lloyd's and Betty's Christmas gifts to one another, and she had taken them at the last minute, just in case they didn't make it back in time for the blessed day.

Once they were satisfied that they had forgotten nothing, the Brickers climbed into the car. Lloyd fired the engine and put some rockabilly Elvis in the eight track.

"Honey, where are we going?" Betty finally thought to ask.

Lloyd thought of his dream. In one disturbing scene, he had watched as a Christmas tree decorated with poker chips fell crashing into a slot machine.

"We're goin' to Vegas," he told Betty. "Let's roll."

And roll they did, leaving the lonely little turquoise-and-white house trailer with its faded contingent of pink flamingo sentinels in a cloud of Arizona desert dust.

They drove through the night. Betty slept, and Lloyd stopped only twice—once to comb his hair, and once to avail himself of God's great outdoor lavatory. By the time the pink light of dawn was lining the eastern horizon, Las Vegas lay shimmering to the west.

Betty began to stir.

"We almost there?" she mumbled, as she wiped a slick patch of sleep drool off her chin.

"Almost," said Lloyd.

"And what are we gonna do, when we get there?"

"Only one thing *to* do, honey," Lloyd answered. "We go lookin' for Santa Claus."

Betty made some sound of acknowledgment, yawned

hugely, and sank back down into unconsciousness. Since midnight, Lloyd had been fighting back sleep with caffeine-packed colas and cherry licorice, and he looked at her with heavy eyes, and envy.

Maybe I oughtta pull over, he thought. *Just to rest my eyes, and stretch out a little.*

Lloyd's thoughts were interrupted when a wavering, translucent image appeared to him, floating just above the hood of the shark. It was his father, in the red velvet suit with white fur trimming, looking just as he had in the dreams. The man leered at Lloyd, through the pitted windshield.

"Boy, I *need* you!" he hollered, over the noise of the road.

"I know, Daddy. I'm comin'," promised Lloyd. "You hang tight," he said, as he grabbed another licorice whip and put the pedal down.

For the first time since he had started having the disconcerting dreams, Lloyd felt full of fire, and hope.

Fifty-three hours later, the fire had been doused, and the situation looked hopeless.

"Please tell me, what was I thinkin'?" he moaned. With a bitter expression, and a falsely bright voice, he lampooned himself.

"Hey, hon! Based upon the highly reliable, albeit likely symbolic, information found in my subconscious mind, let's spend our last dime on a trip to Vegas, so's I can find my long lost Daddy, or a needle in a haystack—whichever comes first!"

"It's not your fault, Lloyd Jr.," said Betty. "No one could have guessed that this would be so hard. Why, personally,

I never would have thought that Las Vegas would have so many shopping centers, and stores, and Santa Clauses. I just never thought of this city having Christmas, the same as everyplace else."

"Well, apparently, it does. And, apparently, I am a dream-chasing fool."

Lloyd was despondent. He lay on the worn chenille spread of the bed in the cheapest motel within the Vegas city limits. His pompadour had gone flat, and he hadn't shaved since the previous day. There was a mustard stain on the piping of his black satin western-style shirt, and he hadn't bothered to change it. For more than an hour, he had been toying with his nearly empty wallet every few minutes, flipping it open to the old photo.

Betty snuggled up beside Lloyd, on the sagging mattress. She touched the corner of the photograph with one long, pink fingernail.

"Handsome," she said. "But not so much as his son."

The compliment didn't cheer Lloyd, but it did draw him out, a little.

"Look at this," he said, and he showed Betty a tiny picture of Elvis Presley, which he had folded to fit in the plastic sleeve against the back of his father's photo. "When I was a kid, I used to pretend that The King was my daddy. That worked pretty good. You know, when I was in a tight spot, or something, I could always imagine what kind of advice he'd give me."

Lloyd took one more look at his real father's picture, and then snapped the wallet closed. He swung his legs over the side of the bed and sat up, with his back to his wife.

"I don't know why, but I had got to thinkin' that a real

daddy might be better," he said, over his shoulder. "Well, I guess I shoulda stuck with Elvis. He never would have advised me to do this. Using up our rent money. Makin' you miss work at the beauty parlor. Goin' on this wild goose chase. Wild *ghost* chase, most likely, because if Lloyd Sr. isn't dead, he's probably at least dead drunk."

Betty knelt behind her husband, and began to knead his shoulders.

"C'mon, now, Lloyd Jr.," she said, softly. "Don't be so hard on yourself. Why don't you lie down again. I have four quarters left for the magic fingers machine."

Lloyd paused for a moment, seeming to consider the therapeutic benefits of spending five minutes on a vibrating bed. But then he shook his head decisively, and stood up. He snatched the quarters out of Betty's outstretched palm.

"I'm keepin' this money, Betty," he said. "I'm savin' it, and I'm gonna spend it in some sensible way. Mark my words, I have squandered my last."

Lloyd shoved the coins into the pocket of his jeans.

"Now let's get packed up," he said. "It's near checkout time, and we're goin' home."

The Brickers checked out of the motel, and then found themselves a pawn shop. Lloyd put his two jade rings and best silver belt buckle on the counter. Betty, avoiding eye contact because she was feeling just a little teary, added her wedding ring to the pile. The man who ran the place looked it all over, and gave them a couple of twenties.

Lloyd didn't have it in him to argue.

"It'll get us home," he said to Betty, as they left the store.

They filled the thirsty Shark's gas tank, and had a few dollars left over.

"I'm buying us lunch," said Lloyd. "Something other than spray cheese. You wait here, and I'll be right back."

Betty nodded. She watched Lloyd walk across the parking lot to a big diner, and rubbed absentmindedly at the indentation on her finger where her ring had once been.

Lloyd walked through the door of the diner, and found it buzzing with noontime traffic. Every vinyl-upholstered booth was stuffed full of customers, and there wasn't a seat to be had at the long, Formica counter. Waitresses in brown-and-white polyester dresses and tennis shoes ran back and forth, between the order window and the patrons, laying down food, pouring coffee, and memorizing orders with practiced ease. The hot smell of burgers, fries and gravy hung heavy in the air.

Lloyd walked up to the cash register and took a menu out of the wire rack that was bolted to the counter beside it. He scanned the selections, and made a quick decision.

"Can I get a couple a' meatloaf sandwiches to go?" he called to the waitress who was nearest to him.

She nodded, turned, and called the order in.

"Two doorstops in a baggie!"

One of the oily-looking short-order cooks yelled, "Got it."

And then there was nothing for Lloyd to do except wait for the food.

He read the headlines of the newspapers that were stacked for sale in front of the counter. He debated whether or not to purchase a package of gum. He had just ducked down a little to check his hair in the warped reflection of the stainless-steel soft ice cream machine, when the door to the men's washroom burst open, behind him. The noise was loud enough to make him look, and what he saw made him straighten up and pay attention.

It was a man in a Santa Claus suit. More specifically a staggering drunk in a Santa Claus suit, reeling from wall, to wall clutching a crumpled brown paper bag to his chest.

A sweaty-looking bald man, wearing a cheap tie, followed close behind him.

"I told you already to get out!" shouted the bald man. "My customers don't want their kids to see this! You're a disgrace, being drunk in that suit!"

Drunken Santa grabbed the counter next to Lloyd for support. He turned around and muttered some incoherent thing to the bald man.

The bald man waved his hand in front of his face, trying to dissipate the cloud of Drunken Santa's stinking breath.

"Yeah, I called the agency, already!" he said. "So don't think you're getting paid a penny! And you shouldn't! You disgrace! Now get out, because I'm going, right now, to call the cops!"

The bald man strode purposefully to the telephone that sat behind the counter. He picked up the receiver and began to push buttons.

"No you don't...Don't do that..." Drunken Santa slurred.

"Excuse me, sir," said Lloyd. Drunken Santa seemed not to hear him.

"No you *don't!*" he raged at the bald man.

"Hello, police?" said the bald man.

"You wouldn't happen to be Lloyd Bricker Sr., would you?" asked Lloyd.

"Two meatloaf sandwiches, hon. Eight-fifty." said the waitress.

"Arrrrgh!" said Drunken Santa, and he picked up a hollow plastic elf, the size of a five-gallon pail, from the tacky Christmas village that decorated the area between the cash register and the washrooms. He pulled his arm back, and launched the cheerful but tacky looking character at the bald man.

Drunken Santa's aim was off by 45 degrees. The elf sailed through the order window that led to the kitchen, and landed on the grill.

"Bah!" he shouted, spraying spittle across the cash register, and counter, and Lloyd. "Bah!"

Then the smell of burning plastic filled the air, and Lloyd Bricker Jr. watched, wide-eyed, as his dream began to unfold.

"Get the elf! Get the elf!" someone screamed.

The happy creature was melting, right through the grill. Where the molten plastic was dripping down, bright flames were beginning to shoot up.

One of the kitchen staff grabbed at the elf and burned his hand. A second later, another man tried to pick the thing up with a towel. When he pulled away, the towel was in flames.

"Dammit!" he yelled, and instinctively flung the burning cloth away from him.

The elf went tumbling to the floor. At that instant,

a waitress opened one of the swinging doors that led to the kitchen, and shrieked when Santa's helper came rolling out across the grubby linoleum, flashing its smoking, liquified face, over and over.

"The tinsel! The tinsel's burning!" someone yelled. There was a whoosh of flame, just above Lloyd's head. He scrambled out of the way just in time to save his hair, and saw a shower of charred garland fall to the countertop.

There appeared to be a great commotion in the kitchen. Through the order window, Lloyd could see half a dozen people rushing around, trying to get the situation under control. The smoke that had been curling out of the window and between the swinging doors was beginning to billow, a fact that was not lost on the majority of the customers.

"The damn kitchen's on fire," hollered one woman, and she pulled her children away from their patty melts and milkshakes and herded them, complaining, toward the door. Others followed. Soon, the crowd was stampeding for the exit, leaving their lunches, and wits, far behind them.

A heavy man in a sweat suit turned to gawk at the flames that had started to lick visibly higher, above the ledge of the order window. As he gaped, he tripped over the candy cane-shaped fence that surrounded the collection of decorative Christmas characters. He came down hard on top of a reindeer, and snapped one of its legs completely off. Santa's normally jolly village mourned its second casualty of the afternoon.

Lloyd's back was pressed hard against the metal edge of the counter. He was trapped by the fleeing crowd, and frozen by his own horror.

"It's my dream," he mumbled to himself, as he stared at the scene. "It's my nightmare."

Just then, a horrified child began to shriek, "Santa Claus! Santa Claus!" and Lloyd turned, knowing exactly what he would see.

Drunken Santa stood several feet away from Lloyd. He appeared to be having the time of his life, laughing diabolically at the havoc he had created with a plastic elf. The child was still screaming, and Lloyd could see why. Drunken Santa was so inebriated, and was enjoying himself so thoroughly, that he had failed to notice a trailing strand of smoldering garland had lit his beard afire. From a smoking patch at the very bottom of the white, synthetic whiskers, a small, orange flame licked out. Lloyd knew that in a second, the man's face would be engulfed in flames.

"*Daddy!*" he heard himself yell. With a mighty push, Lloyd hoisted himself onto the countertop, and across to where Drunken Santa was about to explode into a fat, human torch, cruelly fueled by his polyester suit and synthetic body padding. In one powerful motion, Lloyd gripped the beard, and yanked it away from the man's face. The elastic snapped, just as the fire bloomed. Lloyd yelped, as intense heat singed his wrist, and he tossed the burning thing to the floor. A waitress threw a pot of coffee on top of it, and the flames sputtered harmlessly out.

Lloyd turned, to look at Drunken Santa, unmasked.

It was the face he had seen, in his dreams. It was lined and weathered, beaten by hard living and bad liquor and 30 years' worth of time—but it was still recognizable. It was the face from the photograph in Lloyd's wallet.

Lloyd felt his knees weaken. He felt a tidal wave of emotion washing over him. And he knew what his father was about to say.

"Boy, I need you," the man slurred.

Lloyd felt tears spring to his eyes. He was about to say, *I know, Daddy; I need you, too,* when the man finished his sentence.

"...need you to gimme my hooch," he muttered, and pointed to the counter behind Lloyd.

Lloyd turned to look. The bottle, in its crumpled brown liquor-store bag, had been knocked out of the old man's hand. It lay on the counter, within Lloyd's grasp. He picked it up.

"This?" he asked, and his voice was high, with tension. "*This* is what you needed me for?"

Drunken Santa nodded.

"C'mon. What's keepin' you, boy?" he said.

He doesn't know me, thought Lloyd. Then, on the heels of that thought, came another: *I don't want to know him.*

Lloyd was about to hand the bottle over, but he didn't move fast enough for Drunken Santa. The old man lunged for his precious hooch, grabbed it, and knocked the unsuspecting Lloyd to the ground. He uttered a grunt of satisfaction then, and staggered out the door.

Lloyd lay on the dirty floor by the counter, with his neck bent uncomfortably against the base of a stool.

"I came all this way," he said to himself. If he could have moved his head, he would have shaken it in disbelief.

The sounds coming from the kitchen had become more calm, and the smoke was clearing. The crisis had apparently been averted, although not in time to prevent the mass exit of the diner's lunch crowd. There were no more people sounds to be heard; no conversation, no footsteps, no coughing, or throat-clearing, or slurping or metallic scraping of silverware on plates. Lloyd had begun to think that he was the last customer in the place, when a shiny pair of boots topped by rhinestone-studded pant legs stepped up beside him.

"Oh, man," came a deep, smooth voice from above. "That's a cryin' shame. You alright, son?"

A strong, square hand, adorned with several diamond rings, and a heavy, gold bracelet reached out to Lloyd. He accepted it, and, within a moment, was back on his feet. He had his first good look, then, at the man who had helped him to a standing position.

He was the same height as Lloyd, but a little older and a little heavier. His black hair had been styled into a gravity-defying pompadour, and his eyes were hidden behind an expensive-looking pair of tinted aviator glasses. The rhinestone pattern on his flared pant legs was repeated on the wide collar and yoke of his shirt, and again, on the elaborate, low-slung belt which encircled his slightly paunchy waist. The belt was held together by a massive silver buckle, inset with pieces of jade that formed a scripted letter "E."

The man dusted off Lloyd's shoulder, and offered him a friendly smile. His upper lip had a practiced curl to it.

"Wow," said Lloyd. "Mister, I gotta thank you." He was impressed with the stranger's style, and grateful for his help, and he didn't mind showing it.

"Hey, have I seen you anywhere?" he asked the man. "On TV, maybe? Or do you do your act at one of the fancy hotels, on the strip?" The man was so authentic-looking, Lloyd figured he had to be big-time.

The stranger gave a modest little shrug, and nod.

"Yeah," he said. "I work in the biggest hotel. But I like hangin' out at little joints like this, you hear me? The cheeseburgers are good, and the folks are usually real nice."

"Yeah, I hear you," said Lloyd. There was nothing else to say, then, so he raised his hand in a friendly farewell gesture.

"Well, my wife's waitin'," he said. "I'd best be on my way."

Before he could take two steps toward the door, however, the stranger stopped him.

"Listen, son," he said. "You're lookin' real down in the mouth, and, uh—well, I like the way you do your hair. So let me give you a hot tip. You see that slot machine? The one closest to the door? Well, it's about to pay off. So, you take them four quarters in your pocket, and you put your trust in 'E,' and everything'll work out fine. You'll see."

The stranger clapped Lloyd on the back then, and said, "You take care of yourself, now. And that pretty little Betty of yours, too." Then he walked out the door.

Lloyd blinked once, and lost sight of him. He stood alone, in the destroyed diner, wondering how someone whom he had never before met could have known his wife's name, and the fact that he had exactly four quarters, down deep in the front pocket of his jeans.

Lloyd took the quarters out, and shook them lightly in his closed hand. He looked across the room, to the two worn-looking slot machines that sat next to the door. The diner's scrawny Christmas tree, wittily decorated with poker chips, had been knocked over. The tip of the tree seemed to be pointing to the machine that was closest to the door.

"Well, now, why not," sighed Lloyd. "Everything else about the last 10 minutes has been weird."

He walked over to the machine and took a deep breath.

He plugged the first coin in, and pulled the handle. Nothing.

He plugged the second one in, and pulled the handle. He won nothing.

The third quarter went in, and, again, nothing came out.

Lloyd held up his fourth, and final, quarter.

"This is it," he said, to the machine. "This is my last quarter, and then that's that, because I refuse to spend our lunch money on a one-armed bandit. I have learned my lesson about chasin' crazy notions."

Lloyd put the fourth quarter into the slot then, and pulled the handle.

There was so much noise, he thought for a minute that the diner's fire alarm had finally been triggered.

There were bells, and sirens, and jangling sounds that almost made Lloyd clap his hands over his ears. Mostly, thought, there was the sound of rushing coins, pouring into the bin at the bottom of the machine, and then, when that was full, spilling over onto the floor.

After a moment, Lloyd realized that some of the diner's staff had gathered around to watch.

"Ain't *never* seen one of these machines pay off like that," said a cook in a greasy apron.

"Good for you, hon," said the skinny waitress who had waited on Lloyd. "*Somebody* oughtta have a good day."

Lloyd glanced at the door then, and saw that someone else had witnessed his good fortune. Betty was standing there, her eyes wide and her hands covering the surprised "O" of her mouth.

"Hi, baby," said Lloyd. Then he asked her, "Do you think you could bring me the empty suitcase out of the car?"

Within an hour, after making an important return trip to the pawn shop, they were on the highway. Betty was wearing her wedding ring, once more, and kept waggling it in front of her face, for the pure pleasure of just seeing it.

"I just got so worried, when all those people came running out of the diner," she said. That's why I went over, and that's when I saw the Santa-man, the one you told me about, from your dream."

"I know, honey," said Lloyd.

"And he did, Lloyd, he *did* look like that picture of your daddy, I swear."

"That, he did."

Betty shook her head, and fidgeted in her seat, and twisted her ring around, on her finger. The day had simply been too exciting. A number of scattered thoughts tumbled in her brain. Finally, one took hold.

"You know, Lloyd Jr., you never did tell me if you got to talk to him! Did you meet him, honey? Did you get to meet your daddy?"

"Betty," Lloyd said, "I think I met 'em both. And, I tell you, I'll *never* understand what happened, back there. But I feel different now. I feel finished with it, like I'm my own man, and I don't need to be lookin' for my Daddy, no more."

Betty reached over and stroked Lloyd's cheek.

"Well, that's good," she said.

Lloyd took a deep, thoughtful breath.

"Yes, it is," he agreed. "It would have been nice to have a 'father-son relationship,' but I can accept now that it is just not part of my personal destiny."

Betty looked at Lloyd for a minute. She chewed on her lip, seemingly trying to come to a decision.

"Pull over," she finally said.

"Why?"

"Just do it. Pull over."

Lloyd checked his rear-view mirror, slowed down, and steered the shark over to the wide shoulder of the highway.

"Okay, what?" he said, as he shifted the car into park.

Betty turned around, and began rummaging through the things that were strewn across the car's broad back seat. She found what she was looking for, and handed it to Lloyd with great ceremony.

"Merry Christmas, honey!" she said. It was a small, brightly wrapped gift.

"But, it's not Christmas for two more days," Lloyd said.

"I know. But I think this would be a good time to open it, anyway."

Lloyd shrugged, and smiled, and tore off the shiny paper, with the enthusiasm of a child. He opened the box that was inside, and unfolded what lay within. It was a tiny t-shirt, with a name carefully cross-stitched on the front.

"Now, let's see. It says 'Lloyd Jr., Jr.'" The message sunk in, and Lloyd turned to Betty.

"Are you, for sure?" he asked.

She nodded.

"I've been waitin' to tell you. But I wanted the moment to be just so."

Betty wiped under her eyes, then, and laughed.

"So, you see?" she said, brightly. "You can go ahead and have that father-child relationship—you're just gonna have to do the 'daddy' part!"

"I can do that," Lloyd said, with wonder. He spoke quietly; almost to himself. Then he laughed aloud, and swept Betty into a hug.

"I can do that!" he shouted.

"Yes, you can," said Betty. "But, right now, I think you oughtta drive, Big Daddy, because I'd like to get home before Christmas."

Lloyd let out a war whoop, put the shark in gear, and peeled back onto the highway, leaving a cloud of dust.

The car sped off toward the broad, darkening, eastern horizon.

"I'm gonna teach him to catch!"

"Uh-huh."

"I'm gonna take him fishing!"

"I know you will."

"Hell, I guess I might get even a job. No! No! I'm *definitely* gonna get a job! That's definite!"

"That'd be nice, honey. Real nice," said Betty. She snuggled contentedly down into the seat, then, and Lloyd drove, and together, they watched the stars flicker to life in the vast, desert sky.

Part 3

Miracles

"Where there is great love there are always miracles."

—Willa Cather, *Death Comes for the Archbishop* (1927)

Super Hero

"Superman is stronger."

"Only because of his super powers. But, if he didn't have 'em, Batman would be way tougher. Plus, Batman's got a lot of neat stuff. *And*, he's rich, when he's just being Bruce Wayne."

Eight-year-old Danny Hansen walked along in silence, for a while, considering his older brother's opinion. David was 11, so he knew a lot of stuff.

"What about Captain America?" Danny asked.

David sighed, and rolled his eyes.

"Well, he has super powers, too, but they're the scientific kind. From the super-soldier serum, and the vita-rays."

"Well, I still like Superman," Danny announced, stubbornly.

"I never said *not* to, dummy."

David wasn't allowed to call Danny names, and Danny knew it. But there wasn't much he could do about it when their mother was out of earshot. And even if Danny felt like tattling later on, he couldn't—because the brothers were on a highly secret mission. They were traveling downtown, to the big department stores, to shop for their mother's Christmas present.

David—who had been taking out the garbage for a quarter, every week, and had saved every penny of his birthday money—had six dollars and 73 cents. Danny—who had yet to secure such gainful employment around the house—had $3.25. Together, that was $9.98. That was almost ten dollars, and ten dollars, according to David, was more than enough to buy their mother the nicest gift she had ever received.

With their money stuffed into the pockets of their jeans, they had set out on the Saturday morning, to accomplish their mission. They walked along the winding tree-lined street of the Seattle suburb where they lived, and eventually they came to a main thoroughfare. At the corner, David turned right.

"Where you goin'?" asked Danny, and he pointed to a transit sign that was across the street to their left. "The bus stop is over here."

"Forget about the bus," said David. "We're going to hitch a ride."

Danny was uncertain.

"Mom says we're not supposed to hitch," he said.

"I know that," David said. "But the bus will cost money, and then we won't be able to buy her as nice a present."

"I don't know."

"Okay, look," said David, and he explained his position, with great patience. "If we ride the bus, then we'll have to buy Mom something like soap, or hankies—same as what we get her every year. But if we save the fare, then, I was thinking, we could maybe get her something special. Maybe like an evening gown, like what the ladies on Ed Sullivan wear. She'd like one of those fancy evening gowns, right?"

Danny nodded hesitantly.

"So, this one time, Mom would probably say that hitching is a good idea, right?"

"I guess." Danny didn't feel too sure about it, but it was hard to argue with David's logic. He joined his brother at the edge of the sidewalk, and they both stuck out their thumbs.

It wasn't long before a big delivery truck pulled up to the curb. The driver leaned over and cranked down the passenger-side window.

"You boys headed downtown?" he asked.

"Yes, sir." Danny and David nodded in unison.

"Well," the driver jabbed his thumb in the direction of a "No Riders" sign that sat in the window of the truck, "my boss says I can't let no one ride in the cab of the truck with me. But he didn't say nothin' about the back! You two can hop in with the cargo if you feel like it."

To Danny and David, that sounded like much more fun than a regular ride. They thanked the driver enthusiastically and yanked open the back door. There were a number of boxes in the hold but still plenty of room to sit down.

There was a good-sized sliding window between the cargo hold and the cab, and the driver slid it open a notch.

"Just hafta make one more stop," he yelled, "but I'll have you downtown in no time. You two sit tight now."

Then, with a lurch, the truck pulled back into traffic. The brothers both laughed with delight as their bodies swayed with the rough movement of the vehicle.

"I'm Superman!" yelled Danny, and he stretched his arms out before him as though he was flying.

"I'm Batman!" roared David, and he made his hands into two "V" signs and held them over his eyes like a mask.

The boys whooped and laughed and enjoyed themselves thoroughly for several minutes. They were disappointed when the truck pulled over and stopped at the side of the road.

"We must be on a big hill," said David.

Danny nodded in agreement. His back was pressing heavily against the back wall of the cargo hold. Sure enough, the brothers heard the rusty groan of the hand brake as the driver pulled it on.

A moment later, the back door of the truck opened, and the driver grabbed one of the boxes.

"This is it, fellas. Last stop. I'll be back in a minute."

The driver slammed the door shut then, and the boys were left to wait.

They sat quietly, knowing that there would be no fun in playing super hero until the truck was moving once more. Within a few short minutes, they were fidgety and impatient.

"How long do you think?..." Danny began to ask his older brother, when he was interrupted by a violently loud noise from outside.

There was the blaring of a horn, the ear-piercing squeal of tires, and then the unmistakable sound of metal crunching against metal. Though the boys couldn't see a thing, they could hear that a collision had taken place just behind the truck that they were in.

"Holy cow!" shouted David, and he jumped to his feet. Almost immediately, he was thrown back down, as something huge and heavy slammed into the rear of the truck.

"Ow!" said David, who had hit his head against one of the big cartons.

"They crashed into us, too!" said Danny, with a mixture of fear and excitement. "Wait 'til the driver comes back! Wait 'til he sees that his truck got smashed!"

Suddenly, there was a metallic creaking sound and a jerky movement. Danny and David looked at each other in horror, both realizing at the same time that when the driver came back, he was going to see something much worse than a smashed truck. The driver was going to see a gone truck.

"We're rolling," whispered David. "Holy geez, we're rolling down the hill!"

Once again, the brothers felt themselves being tossed about by the motion of the vehicle. But it was more violent than it had been before, more out of control. And the speed was increasing steadily.

"I'm scared David! I'm scared!" Danny cried out.

The trucked careened down the hill, and the ride grew wilder by the minute. The big, heavy cartons slid back and forth across the floor of the truck. Smaller ones were tossed here and there as the truck pitched and rolled. The terrified boys clung to one another, and David did something which he had never done aloud, especially in front of his little brother. He prayed.

"Please, God!" he sobbed. "I promise I won't ever do another bad thing, and I'll listen to my mom, and I don't even care if I don't get that new sled for Christmas! Please save us, now, and I'll be real good, I promise!"

And suddenly, the truck lurched to the right and slowed a little.

"Don't panic, boys!" called a voice from the cab. "Just hang on tight! I'm trying to jam the brakes on now!"

Danny and David stared at one another. Their eyes were wide, and their jaws hung open.

"Did you hear that?" whispered Danny.

"I heard, I heard," said David.

That meant that it couldn't have been their imaginations. Also, the truck seemed to be moving in a more controlled fashion than it had before. Though it continued to speed down the hill, there was less reeling and rocking. Impossibly, someone seemed to be guiding the hurtling vehicle along its dangerous path.

And suddenly, the boys' curiosity was greater than their fear.

"Let's look," said David, in a low voice. Danny nodded, although it was barely perceptible given the jostling motion of the truck.

The brothers carefully got to their feet and crouched behind the sliding window that led to the cab. As they clung to the wall to keep their balance, David used his fingernails to pry the panel open.

What they saw stunned them.

The cab of the truck was empty—absolutely empty. Yet the steering wheel moved in a controlled and deliberate manner, turning to avoid a car at one point, holding straight and true to avoid a group of horrified pedestrians at another. When there was a curve in the road, the truck navigated it perfectly. And when a distracted woman nearly stepped off the curb to cross the street in front of the runaway vehicle, Danny and David watched as the horn ring in the center of the steering wheel depressed three times, giving three loud warning blasts.

"What's going on, David?" Danny asked.

David simply shook his head. All he knew for sure was that if he made it home that night, he would give his mother no argument about attending church the following morning.

The incline became less severe eventually, and the delivery truck slowed. Finally, at the bottom of the hill, it rolled to a lazy stop and bumped gently against the side of the curb.

"You're safe, now," the voice said. The words had a strange, hollow quality, and Danny and David couldn't tell exactly where they were coming from. But, before they had time to think about it, there were many more voices—all frantic, all coming from the crowd that was gathering outside of the truck.

"Oh my God! Did you see that?"

"I can't believe there wasn't a *huge* accident. I just can't believe it!"

"It missed my car by just *that* much!"

The boys had just stood up on shaking legs when they heard a man say, "Look, here comes the driver now."

A moment later, the back door of the truck was yanked open, and the fellow who had been good enough to give them a ride stood there. The man's cheerful expression was gone; his face had become a pale mask of fear. When he saw Danny and David standing, unharmed, in the middle of his cargo bay, he nearly collapsed with relief.

"Oh, thank the good Lord!" he said, as he wiped the perspiration from his face with a trembling hand. "I never would have forgiven myself, never in a day. Come on out now, you two. Outta there, now."

When the brothers stepped down out of the delivery truck, there were gasps of shock.

"There were *children* in there?" said one woman, and her hands fluttered to her face.

"You two fellas alright, now?" asked a tall man, who crouched down to the boys' level.

Danny and David both nodded. The driver clapped each of them on the back.

"They're more than alright," he said. "They're quick thinkin' and scared of nothin'."

The driver turned to face the brothers then, and gave them a sincere look of admiration.

"I hate to think what woulda happened, if you hadn't crawled through the window to grab that wheel."

Danny and David looked at one another.

"Well, sir," said David. "The thing is, we didn't."

"What?" said the driver. "What do you mean, boys?"

Danny spoke up, then.

"We were in the back, the whole time," he said. "We didn't steer the truck."

"Well, someone did!" declared the driver with certainty.

"No, those two boys are telling the truth," said a large man, who was standing in the crowd. "I was watching that truck, and there was no one in the cab. There were no hands on that steering wheel, and no one got out when it came to a stop here."

There was a hush, then, until finally, one little old lady spoke to her friend.

"It's like a Christmas miracle," she said, and there were murmurs of agreement throughout the crowd.

While the driver was examining his delivery truck and scratching his head, and the bystanders were all talking amongst themselves about miracles and luck and the strangeness of fate, Danny and David decided to slip away.

"Let's go now, before someone wants to drive us home," whispered David. "That way, Mom doesn't have to know."

Danny thought that sounded sensible, and he followed his brother quietly through the crowd, and around the corner of the nearest building.

When they were safely out of sight of the group, they each sighed with relief.

"Bus?" asked Danny, as they approached a bench with a transit sign.

"Oh, yeah!" said David. "Absolutely."

The brothers sat down. They waited in silence for a moment, and then Danny spoke.

"You know," he said, "Superman and Batman are both neat, but the Invisible Man is great, too."

"Yeah!" said David, with a burst of tension-relieving laughter. "The Invisible Man was fantastic!"

The brothers laughed together then until their sides ached and tears streamed down their faces, and the bus came to take them downtown.

The Debt

The woman's name was Yvonne. She stood in her living room, with a friend, examining her Christmas tree without enthusiasm.

The decorating attempt had been half-hearted at best, and it showed. Most of the ornaments still rested in their boxed nest of shredded paper, and the ones that had been hung from the tree's branches had been put on without much thought or care.

"It could really use something at the top," said the friend.

"No," Yvonne said, bluntly. "Putting the star on was always Owen's job. I really don't want to look at that star for the next two weeks."

The friend was understanding and said nothing more. Owen had been Yvonne's only child, and he had died, only the month before.

Owen had been a young man, living his own life in Toronto, when he had discovered that he was terminally ill. Before long, he had moved back to his mother's modest little home in Timmins.

"I want to be near you, Mom," he had told Yvonne, "and it would help me to not have so many expenses."

Yvonne eventually learned that Owen was worried about his financial situation because of a debt that he carried. He was able to make the monthly payment but worried that he might not live long enough to pay the amount in full.

One night, as mother and son sat up talking, Owen expressed his concern.

"I've always paid my bills," he told Yvonne. "It's just the decent, honest thing to do. But I'm really worried about this one. What if I die before the loan is paid up?"

Yvonne took a deep breath. She wanted to tell Owen that she would handle it, but they both knew that she didn't have the money. She had been a single mother and had always worked hard. She had given Owen a good education, and she owned her house, but she had a limited income and no savings to dip into. Finally, Yvonne told Owen the one thing that she believed to be true of difficult situations.

"You do your best," she told her son, "and God will take care of the rest."

Owen had smiled at the saying which he had often heard while growing up.

"I hope so, Mom," he had said. "I'd sure hate to be remembered as a deadbeat."

"That could never happen, never," said Yvonne. And before she went to sleep that night, she prayed that she was right.

Two weeks later, on a gray November day, Owen had died. As much as he had not wanted to, he left his mother alone, and his debt unpaid.

Yvonne was devastated. She withdrew from life. As November turned into December, it became apparent to her friends and co-workers that she was in no way celebrating the holiday season.

"Do a little something," a concerned friend urged her.

"Remember what Christmas is really about. You've always had a strong faith, and you need it more than ever now."

Finally, Yvonne allowed one of her friends to persuade her to put up the Christmas tree. But afterward, she felt worse instead of better. As she lay in bed that night, she came to a decision.

I can't avoid it any longer, she thought. *Tomorrow, I'm going to start sorting out Owen's finances.*

Early the next morning, Yvonne sat at her kitchen table with a shoe box full of records and receipts. On one piece of paper, she had written the outstanding amount of Owen's debt. On another, she was adding up his meager assets.

As lunch-time approached, however, Yvonne was beginning to think that Owen's assets were not quite as limited as he had thought. The little amounts of money from various sources were adding up to a significant number.

Owen had left a little bit of cash in a bank account. Yvonne noted it down. He had kept careful records of checks that were owed to him. Yvonne added each one to the list. There had been an insurance package, too—one with quite a small benefit, but it was all adding up. By the end of the day, Yvonne was encouraged.

"Owen, it won't be enough to pay the debt," she said, aloud, "but it's a good start. It's a step in the right direction."

Yvonne spent the next day on the telephone, arranging to have Owen's assets sent to her. The man at the insurance company had given her a bit of good news.

"There will be some interest added to the sum you have," he told her. "I'm not sure how much, but you can expect more."

As it turned out, almost every check and money order that eventually arrived was for an amount just slightly greater than what Yvonne had expected. When the last of them came in a few days before Christmas, Yvonne added up the numbers excitedly.

The total came to exactly $3.89 more than the outstanding amount on Owen's loan. Yvonne smiled, and thought to herself that it was the best Christmas gift she could have possibly received.

She went to the post office that very evening and stood in the long line-up with all the people who were sending packages and cards off to their loved ones. It made her miss Owen, but she didn't allow herself to give in to melancholy. In a way, Yvonne reasoned, she *was* sending a gift for her son.

The minutes ticked by, and the line moved slowly, and, finally, it was Yvonne's turn to be served. She walked up to the counter and wrote a number down on a piece of paper.

"I'd like a money order for this amount, please," she said, "and I'll need one stamp."

The clerk nodded, and went about printing up the money order. She slid a single stamp across the counter to Yvonne. Then she rang the order up on the till.

"Okay," she said. "On top of the amount of the money order, there's the *price* of the money order itself, and the stamp. With tax, that comes to..."

"Wait!" Yvonne said, suddenly. "Don't tell me! An extra $3.89—right?"

The clerk nodded.

"Three-eighty-nine," she confirmed. "You've got a good head for numbers, ma'am."

Later that evening, Yvonne stood in her living room, looking at the sad, ignored, little Christmas tree. She had pulled the box of ornaments out of the closet once more and had decided that she would do a proper job of decorating.

She strung the lights up first, and plugged them in. She added more garland and more baubles. She took the bows and bells that had already been on the tree and rearranged them in a more attractive fashion. Then, all that was left was the star.

Yvonne took the elaborate ornament of white and gold glass out of its box and held it gently in her hands. She remembered all the years when Owen had placed it, carefully, at the top of the tree. Tears sprang to Yvonne's eyes, and, for a moment, she thought that she would have to put the star away until the following year.

"But that wouldn't be right," she said to herself. As painful as it was going to be, Yvonne wanted to spend Christmas with at least the memory of Owen.

She stood on top of the step stool, and put the star on the tree. Then she got down and took a few steps backward, so she could see the effect.

It looked lovely.

"Owen, you'll always be my star," she said. "I sure wish you were here."

Yvonne turned then to gather up the empty boxes and return them to the closet. That was when she realized that Owen *was* there, with her.

The star had always been stored in its original package, with the faded, peeling price tag on the upper righthand corner of the clear plastic cover. Yvonne had never paid

much attention to that price tag before, but as she picked the box up that year, it caught her attention. More than her attention—it made her catch her *breath*—because it held a certain message from Owen.

The amount that they had paid for the Christmas star, years and years before, was exactly three dollars, and 89 cents.

Grandfather's Clock

By two o'clock, Vi Wesson figured that she was ready for the party.

She'd spent all the previous day cleaning her house, and it was in a near-spotless state. The food had all been made that very morning and was sitting in the refrigerator on fancy trays, under stretched sheets of plastic wrap. The Christmas tree had been decorated a week earlier, and the gifts that had been wrapped a month earlier and purchased back during the summer were stacked beneath it. Vi even had her hair set and her minimal amount of makeup applied, and the outfit that she planned to wear—the green wool slacks, with the new, cream silk blouse—was hanging on the peg behind her bedroom door.

Everything was ready, with hours to go. So when the clock-repair fellow arrived, to fix Big Len, she had all the time in the world to chat with him.

"It was sort of a joke, you know. My late husband's name was Leonard, and it was his clock, so we called it 'Big Len,' after the one in England, like. You heard of that famous clock in England? Big Ben?"

The clock repairman, who was opening his case of tools and parts on the freshly vacuumed carpet, glanced at Vi and nodded.

"Course you have," said Vi. "You're a clock expert, aren't you. You want tea, or coffee, maybe?"

The repairman looked briefly at Vi once more, this time with a shake of his head.

"No, thanks, ma'am," he said.

"Suit yourself," she said. She settled down into a dining room chair that was close to where the man was working and lit a cigarette. There was nothing like having a nice visit along with a cigarette.

"My gosh!" Vi said, as she looked over the man's selection of instruments. "You sure have to carry a lot of doodads!"

"Well," said the repairman, "you can never tell what you might need. Now, what's the problem with this clock?"

"My husband died."

The repairman looked confused at first, then uncomfortable.

"That's a shame," he finally said, in a voice that was just a shade louder, and a bit slower than usual. "But about the *clock?*" he asked, and he patted the walnut case of the antique grandfather clock for clarity.

"Oh, I'm not slow," said Vi, and she blew out a stream of smoke. "I'm not crazy, neither. The problem with the clock is that my husband is dead. But I was hoping you might be able to do something about that. The clock, that is; not Leonard. Lord knows I loved him, but the state he'd be in now, I don't want him back, thank you very much."

The repairman scratched his head and tried to follow Vi's stream-of-consciousness conversation.

"Okay—the clock doesn't work at all?" he asked.

"Not a tick," said Vi, and she flicked the ash from her cigarette into the ashtray that sat next to her wrist, on the table with the lace tablecloth. "It's not slow, or fast, or anything. It just doesn't go. So I thought I'd try, one more time, to get it fixed up, because I'm having the family for a Christmas party tonight, and my daughters—I've got two of them, there's Sandra and Gaylene—they'd sure like to see that clock running again."

The repairman examined the wood panels of the old clock, and then gently opened the case. A layer of fine dust had settled on the inner workings.

Vi shook her head.

"Doesn't matter how much you clean," she said. "There's always something that still *needs* a cleaning."

"So, you said you've had other people try to fix this?"

"Two times," said Vi, and she held up two fingers for emphasis. "They couldn't find a damn thing, pardon my French. Said there was no reason it shouldn't be running. And they were supposed to be a couple of the best clock-makers in Winnipeg, 'skilled craftsmen,' that's what Sandra said. But I figure they couldn't fix it, because they didn't know what was really wrong with it. So that's why I called you, and that's why I'm telling you, up front, that the clock isn't working, because Leonard's dead. So now that you know that, you can do whatever it is that you have to do, in that kind of a situation."

"Look, ma'am," the repairman said, "I just don't understand what you're getting at, here. Maybe I should go." He started to fold up his tool kit.

"I'll pay you cash, over and above," said Vi.

"What do you mean?"

"I mean, I'll pay the bill that your boss sends me, but I'll also give you a 50-dollar bill all your own, if you can fix this."

The repairman took a good long look at Vi Wesson then, and tried to size her up. She seemed very serious and not particularly crazy, despite the things which she had been saying.

"That's a pretty big tip," said the repairman.

"It's worth it to me," said Vi. She stubbed out her cigarette and went into the kitchen. The repairman heard the china clink of a sugar bowl lid, and Vi returned to the dining room with a crisp, 50-dollar bill.

"My Sandra, she's got a baby on the way. And, for a present, I'd like to give her the clock. It's an heirloom, and Leonard would have wanted it passed down. But there's not much point in it, if the damn thing won't work."

"I suppose," said the repairman. He had his eye on the 50. He was thinking that he could buy his kid a new computer game to put under the tree. He was thinking *that* would show his ex-wife who the better parent was.

Vi saw the man looking at the money and knew that she had a deal. She pressed the bill into his hand.

"Here you go," she said. "In advance. Now, why don't you let me get you that coffee, and then I'll tell you exactly what happened to Big Len."

Five minutes later, Vi and the repairman were both seated at the dining room table. Each held a mug of steaming coffee, and a plate of frosted sugar cookies sat between them.

"You can eat all of those that you want," said Vi, as she snapped her lighter open, and put the flame to the tip of another cigarette. "I've got fancier ones saved for the party." She stared expectantly at the repairman, and the cookies until, finally, he took one.

"Thanks," he mumbled, and took a small bite.

"Oh, that's fine," said Vi. "I like to feed you young people, although you're too much for the sweets, I can tell you. A little bit of fruit and a little sugar in my coffee is all I need."

"You were going to tell me what happened to the clock?"

"Yeah, the clock," said Vi, and she turned slightly, and looked it up and down. "It's beautiful, hey? Beautiful old antique. It's been in the Wesson family longer than any living Wesson. Always belonged to the oldest male heir.

"And, you know, it's funny," she continued. "I don't know too much about my own family. Not too much of the history, like. But Len, he told stories about his folks, all the time. It was important to him, all of that history that the Wessons had. So now, I know it better than my own. I was married to Len for 35 years, and ended up being more of a Wesson than I ever was a Clarke. That was my maiden name—Clarke. Now, if I was waiting in the doctor's office, and the nurse came out and called for "Violet Clarke," I wouldn't even look up from my magazine.

"Now, the clock—I think the one who bought it was Len's great grandfather, but I'm not a hundred per cent sure on that. What I do know for sure is that his grandfather, John Wesson, brought it with him when he and his bride came out from Ontario. Everyone said they were crazy to be lugging such a thing out to the frontier. This was 1890, you know, and Winnipeg was a pretty decent-sized little burg, but you couldn't tell that to anyone who lived in the east.

"Anyway, John and Kate Wesson were new-married, and this clock was a wedding gift from his father, and he had his mind set that it was going with them. So they paid the freight, and John and Kate and the grandfather clock all came out here together, on the CPR.

"Now, when they got here, they were in for a shock. There were a lot of people in those days, but the sort of civilization that John Wesson was used to hadn't quite caught up with all of them. From what I heard, parts of the city was no more than a scattered-out collection of rough shacks and between 'em was mud streets that got baked hard and dusty in the summertime and got as sticky and mucky as a bog, come wet weather.

"John and Kate hadn't been here more than a few days when they got a feel for that mud. They'd just got themselves a place to live, so they loaded up all of their things into a cart, and they left The Royal Hotel and made their way out to this little house. Well, the further away from Main Street they got, the softer and muckier the road got. Finally, about a quarter-mile from the house, the cart got stuck so bad, they couldn't budge it another inch.

"So John says to Kate, 'We'll just have to pack everything the rest of the way.' And they did. They made trip after trip, wading through the mud, and carried in everything except this clock here. They couldn't carry the clock by themselves, and the sun was going down. So they knew they couldn't find anyone to help 'em 'til the next day.

"So *Kate* says, 'C'mon, let's go to bed, and we'll figure this out tomorrow.' But John Wesson wouldn't hear of it. He told her to go on to the house, and he settled himself down in the cart next to the clock. Do you believe that? Not even a week in Winnipeg—which was a rough place, mind you—and he lets his wife sleep alone, so's he can protect this clock.

"Later, one of his boys asked him how he could have done that, and he said he was trying to bring some civilization to this God-forsaken hole.

"By the time John and Kate got truly settled and had their family, it wasn't such a God-forsaken hole, anymore. They had proper streetcar service and milk delivery every morning. The clock probably didn't stick out like such a sore thumb, anymore.

"All those kids heard about the clock, though. They heard the story of how it was passed down to their dad, and how it came out west on a train, wrapped tight in a patchwork quilt. Those kids knew that the clock was part of their heritage, you know, and that, someday, it would go to John Jr.

"But here's what happened: before the old man died, John Jr. died. He went away to serve in the First World War, you know, and he never came back. So the clock eventually went to the other son, and that was the first Leonard Wesson.

"By the time that Leonard was old enough to serve, well, the war was over. Everything was finished. So he got himself a good job, instead, and a wife—her name was Florence. They settled down and started having babies, and *my* Leonard was one of 'em. Leonard Jr.

"I think things were okay for them for the first few years. But then the Depression hit, and it hit Leonard Wesson Sr. particularly hard, because his good job happened to be at one of the big banks that was on Portage Avenue. He lost that job, and when he was lucky enough to work, after that, it was at things that didn't bring in nearly the money or the prestige. I know he sold door-to-door, for a while. Spices and what-have-you, household gadgets. But people weren't buying many spices, when they couldn't afford the food to put underneath 'em.

"I guess, one time, when things were at their worst, Florence said to Len Sr., 'I know a fellow who would pay us quite a few dollars for the clock, and then we could put a decent meal into the children, for once.' Leonard Sr. just flat-out refused. I guess they had a bit of a go-round. And that night—my hubby was about 10 years old, then, so he remembered it just so—the whole family sat around in their worn clothes, sharing a couple of fried potatoes, while that grandfather clock chimed away like they were sitting at the Ritz.

"I wished I met Len Sr. I think he must've been a character. But he died in 1960, a couple of years before Len and I got together. So, you see, when I met up with Len, he already had the clock. It had already got passed down to him.

"I was 25 years old when Len and me got married, and he was about 40. My mother didn't think too much of that. 'If he was old, and had some *money*,' she used to say. 'But he's just *old*.' She thought I'd have a better time with someone more my own age. But Len was good to me, which was more than I could say for some of my own relatives at the time, so I just went right ahead.

"My mother was right about the money, though. We didn't have too much, at first. When we were saving for this place, we lived in a couple of tiny, little apartments, where you had to climb up three flights of stairs with the groceries, and the laundry. I don't ever miss that, I tell you. It'd be so hot in the summertime, I wished I could just walk around naked—pardon my saying so—and the flies would be buzzing, just constant; enough to drive you crazy. And there was hardly room for anything useful, let alone this old clock. But every place we lived, it had to be there.

"One time, I remember, when we just had Sandra, Len and me had a huge fight about that clock. Sandra was about three, I guess, and she'd been making pictures with her crayons. I guess she ran out of paper, after a while, though, because she started drawing on the floor. Then she moved to the wall, and then, just before Len caught her, she made one tiny little line on the base of the grandfather clock.

"Well, Lord! You'd have thought she'd committed a murder! Len gave her a walloping—only time ever, as I recall—and then he sat her down and delivered this roaring lecture about the importance of the clock.

"After a while, I'd had enough. I said to him, 'Len, you leave her alone, now. She's your child. That bloody clock is just a thing.' Well, I tell you. I never said anything like *that* again. Not that he said anything or did anything much—but the look he gave me just stopped me in my tracks. I knew then that however he felt about that clock, I just didn't understand it. And I let it be. Sometimes that's the only thing to do.

"We had Gaylene a little while after that. And then I asked Len if he wanted another baby. But he said 'no.' He was almost 50 then, and I think the very thought of having another little baby bawling all night long made him feel wore out. So we quit after the two girls, then. That was our family.

"I was always happy with that, you know. I had my daughters to do things with. But sometimes I wondered if Len would have been happier with a son. I wondered if we should've tried one more time, for a boy. But when I asked him, he said no, he was just fine, and satisfied. But that was Len. He didn't complain much.

"It was that lack of complaining that did him in, I think. By the time we knew he had cancer, it was everywhere. That's what the doctors said—that it was so many places, there was no point in doing an operation, or chemo, or anything.

"It ended up, we just brought him home. He stayed here for a few weeks, until me and the girls couldn't keep him comfortable anymore. Then he went to the hospital. That was two years ago, right about this time.

"I used to spend hours and hours at that hospital. Even at the end, when everybody told me that he didn't know I was there. I didn't believe that. I knew it made a difference. But, anyway, I couldn't be there every minute, and one day, I came home for a little while, to change my clothes and have a nap in my own bed.

"I walked in the door and sat down in that chair—that green swivel-rocker, right there—and I closed my eyes for a minute. It was so peaceful, like, to be here where it was quiet. Where there was no hospital noise. All I could hear was the hum of the fridge motor, and the tick-tock of Len's grandfather clock.

"So I was sitting there, and I was almost asleep, I think, and suddenly, that clock stops ticking. It froze—just like that. It stopped making noise, and the pendulum, there, stopped swinging, and the hands weren't moving around anymore. And I had a bad feeling, a real dark kind of bad feeling. Then the phone rang, and I knew it was going to be someone from the hospital, telling me that Len had died."

"And was it?" The repairman's coffee cup was empty, and the front of his shirt was dusted with the dry crumbs of Vi's homemade sugar cookies. He didn't notice. He was wrapped up in the story.

"Oh, yeah. He was dead alright. And the clock hasn't ticked a beat since. None of those 'skilled craftsmen' of Sandra's can figure out what's wrong with it, but I know."

"What?"

"Well," said Vi, and she swept a few crumbs from the tablecloth into her hand, and deposited them into the ashtray. "Well, I think it's because it doesn't belong to anyone anymore. The clock was always important to the Wesson men. The women never cared as much for it. And now, there are no more Wesson men."

The repairman looked at the grandfather clock and at his tool case, spread out on the carpet beside it. Then, he looked at Vi.

"I don't think I can fix that," he said.

Vi nodded. There was a little sadness in her eyes.

"I suppose I didn't really expect that you could," she said. "But you can keep the money."

"What for?" The repairman wanted the 50, but didn't want to take it, unfairly.

Vi shrugged.

"You can keep it because you listened to my story. I never told it to anyone, before now."

Just then, the telephone rang. Both Vi and her guest jumped a little at the sound.

"Oh, boy!" she said, nervously. "Who's that, now? Better not be someone saying they can't make it to the party!"

She scurried off to answer the telephone in the hall, and left the repairman sitting by himself.

The man took another long look at the clock, and shook his head. Then he knelt down on the carpet, and began to fold up his tool case.

He could hear the hum of the refrigerator. He could hear the muted, unintelligible words of Vi Wesson's telephone conversation. And, as he snapped the case shut, he heard something else.

It was a groaning—the rusted, mechanical groaning of something that had sat still for a long time, something that was attempting to wrench itself into action. The noise came from the grandfather clock.

The repairman looked up in time to see the case of the clock shudder. Then, there was a moment of silence. And then, the rhythmic ticking began, and the pendulum started to swing.

The repairman jumped to his feet and took several steps away from the clock.

"Ma'am?" he began to call out, before remembering that his hostess was busy on the phone.

The clock was ticking steadily, and at exactly the right speed. The pendulum moved smoothly, as though it had not suffered two years of strange paralysis. The repairman watched in wonder and let out a little laugh.

It was then that Vi walked back into the room. Her face was flushed, and her eyes were bright.

"Well, I don't know what you're laughing about, young fella, but I just got some good news! That was my son-in-law, Martin. He's got hair down to his behind, but he's a good sort. He just told me that Sandra had the baby! It's a little early, and now there's two people not coming to my party, but everyone's healthy and fine."

"Oh, that's nice. I'm glad to hear that," said the repairman, and then he pointed to the clock.

"And look at this, Mrs. Wesson! Your clock's working again!"

Vi Wesson looked at the grandfather clock. Her jaw dropped, and, for a moment, she appeared stunned. But then began to laugh.

"Then I guess I don't have to tell you," she said, when she finally stopped, and caught her breath.

"Tell me what?"

"Sandra's baby," said Vi. *"It's a boy."*

The Warning

Tanya had a cinnamon stick in her cup of hot chocolate and was enjoying the aroma that was wafting from her mug as much as the rich, sweet taste of the drink.

"Have I mentioned that this is perfect?" she asked Kevin.

Kevin smiled. He knew that his wife was talking about more than her beverage. She was talking about everything—the whole experience of spending Christmas Eve at the cabin. And he agreed with her, 100 percent. It was perfect.

"So tell me again why we live in the city?" he asked her. Sometimes, when they were enveloped in the peace and quiet of their little home away from home, he couldn't remember. Edmonton was only a little more than an hour south of the five acres that they owned near Perryvale. But, in a very real sense, it was a world away.

During the week, life was a race that seemed impossible to win—even though Tanya and Kevin were armed with two vehicles and a home with every time-saving aid and they lived in the center of seemingly endless amenities and 24-hour convenience. On weekends, however, the pace slowed. Because they spent their weekends at the acreage, a place where it was impossible to rush, they had time to enjoy each other and the world around them.

They couldn't "jump in the shower" in the morning, because there wasn't a shower. There was no bathroom at all and no running water. They couldn't "run down to the store," or "zip to the mall," because shopping for most

things required a half-hour drive to either Westlock or Athabasca. And when the little log house got a bit chilly, they couldn't turn up a thermostat dial and achieve an instant result. Heating the place meant hauling in wood and coal and stoking up the fires in the cast-iron cooking stove that dominated the large kitchen and in the pot-bellied heater that ruled the living room.

There was electricity—the one concession to modern convenience—which Kevin and Tanya especially enjoyed during the Christmas season. It meant that they could have lights on the tree and outside the cabin—strung in a line beneath the low, sloping roof and running around the crooked little windows. The pretty blue bulbs were the only ones twinkling for more than a mile, and always looked magical, set against the backdrop of pristine snow. It was the kind of snow that one only ever saw in the country, snow that hadn't been soiled by tires, exhaust and dirt. Christmas-card snow, Tanya always thought, comparing it to the painted pictures of idyllic settings that arrived in their mailbox every December.

"Can't think of a reason?" asked Kevin.

"Oh! Sorry," Tanya had been lost in her comfortable reverie and had forgotten to answer Kevin's question.

"Well, let's see," she said. "I suppose there's your job. Living out here full-time *would* make for a bit of a daunting commute. And your mother would throw a fit if we moved Sadie away from her on any permanent basis."

Sadie was the couple's 10-week-old daughter. She had been asleep since early that evening in her portable crib in the bedroom.

"Yeah, but we could do this every night," said Kevin, and he slipped an arm around Tanya's shoulders and pulled her in close.

"You can do that all you want," said Tanya, as she snuggled into her husband's embrace. "I'm getting kind of cold."

"Now that you mention it..." said Kevin, and he glanced over at the big wood and coal heater. The fire appeared to be burning well, but there was a definite chill in the room.

"I bet the fire in the kitchen stove has gone out," he said. "I'd better stoke it up." He jumped up off the sofa and walked into the next room.

The fire was still burning in the big cast-iron stove, but it was a bit low. Kevin lifted one of the round lids from the stove top and threw in a few pieces of split wood. Then he stirred the embers and waited until yellow flames were licking hungrily at the new fuel. By the time he returned to the living room, the fire was already beginning to crackle enthusiastically.

Tanya had taken the afghan that was draped over the rocking chair and had wrapped it around her shoulders.

"I'm freezing," she announced. "And I don't think Santa Claus will stop here, if there's ice forming on top of the eggnog. Can you do something?"

"Relax," said Kevin. "I just got the kitchen fire going really well, and I'll add a scoop of coal to this monster. I promised you a warm and cozy Christmas Eve experience, and I plan to deliver."

He added fuel to the fire in the big heater then, and stood watching as it began to roar.

"You wanted heat, you've got heat," he told Tanya. "In a few minutes, you'll have so much heat, you'll be peeling your clothes off."

"You wish," she retorted. Kevin had to admit, with the way Tanya was shivering under her layers, that it didn't look likely. And, until the two stoves really started to throw off some heat, he needed a little extra warmth himself.

"Can I share?" he asked, as he sank back into his spot on the sofa.

Tanya nodded and wrapped the loose edge of the afghan around him.

As they huddled together under the wrap, Kevin had a sudden thought.

"Sadie!" he said. "Shouldn't we put another blanket on her?"

Tanya considered it.

"She's wearing those really thick, fleece pyjamas," she

said. "And she has three warm blankets tucked around her. I can't imagine that she'd be getting cold, and I don't want to risk waking her up."

"Good point," said Kevin. He loved being a new dad, but quiet times alone with Tanya had become a rare pleasure.

"So, what should we do?" he asked. "Sing carols? Recite *The Night Before Christmas?* Open some presents?"

"No presents until morning!" said Tanya. "Man, you're worse than a kid. And, anyway, I'm starting to think that we'll have to burn the Christmas presents, just to stay alive."

"Could you be more dramatic?" Kevin asked. But, in fact, even he was starting to wonder when the stoves would start putting out some noticeable heat. If anything, he felt even colder than he had prior to stoking the fires. His toes were growing numb inside his thick, wool socks, and he was toying with the idea of putting on a wool hat. Instead, he got up to check the state of the fires.

He went over to the big wood and coal heater first and opened the metal grate. Inside, the flames crackled and popped and filled the belly of the stove. Inches away, Kevin shivered and wondered how many degrees away he was from being able to see his breath.

Tanya was curious about the strange situation, too. With her afghan draped around her like a toga, she wandered over to one of the living-room windows.

"Well, here's our problem," she said.

Kevin looked and saw her holding her hand up, following the shape of the frame.

"There's a serious draft, here," she said.

Kevin shook his head, and held his hand up, next to his wife's.

"But I insulated those windows really well, last fall!" he said. "I stuffed insulation into all the chinks in the logs, and that's heavy-duty plastic that I put over the glass."

Tanya shrugged.

"Well, it doesn't feel like it. Maybe it's really blowing outside."

"I don't hear anything," said Kevin. "And look." He came over to where Tanya was standing and gazed out the window. "If there is a wind, it's not moving those trees."

It was true: the tall poplars that surrounded the yard were standing still and quiet against the starry sky.

"Well, I don't know. This is freaky." Tanya was no longer experiencing her perfect Christmas Eve, and it was making her cranky. She went into the kitchen to put her empty hot chocolate mug on the counter.

By the window over the countertop, she paused. She held out her hand again and looked confused.

"Kevin," she said, "this is really strange."

"What?" Kevin followed her into the kitchen, grabbing his wool hat off the peg by the door as he passed it.

"The wind. The draft. Whatever you want to call it. I can feel it here, too."

"And?"

"Well, even if there was a wind outside—and, if there is, I can't see any evidence of it—wouldn't it be blowing in one direction?"

"Presumably. Your point?"

Tanya looked at her husband in exasperation.

"Well, this window is on the wall opposite *that* window! *That's* my point!"

Kevin stopped then. He thought for a moment and then walked over to the counter. He ran his hand along the frame of the window first and then moved over to the kitchen door. It felt as though a front of frigid air was pressing through the very wall of the cabin. As soon as his hand was within 10 inches of the wall, the air around it felt bone-numbingly cold.

He paused, and frowned.

"Over there, in the living room, it was, like, five inches," he said.

He ran back into the living room, to the place where he had stood minutes earlier. He held his hand up and pushed it forward towards the window, until he felt the wall of invisible ice.

"Ten inches, this time," he whispered. "Maybe more." The words left his mouth with a little plume of condensation.

Kevin heard Tanya shout his name then, and he ran back into the kitchen. He found his wife staring at the cast-iron stove.

"What's going on, here?" she said, and her voice was high and shaky.

Kevin followed her gaze, and understood why.

Inside the stove, the fire was raging. Kevin had put in more wood than he probably should have, and parts of the stove were beginning to glow cherry-red. It was the top of the stove that Tanya was staring at, though, the top of the stove where they kept a basin filled with water so that they could always get a dipper-full of warm water with which to wash their hands.

The water in the basin should have been near boiling. Instead, a wafer-thin sheet of ice had begun to form across the top.

Kevin put his hand close to the stove top. He brought it down, closer. And closer. Finally, he touched the black, cast-iron surface.

It was cool to the touch, but it made Kevin recoil, as though he'd been burned.

"What the *hell* is going on here?!" he yelled, and then walked over to the closest exterior wall. He held his hand up, moved it slowly toward the wall, and stopped when he hit cold air.

"What's that?" he asked Tanya, hysterically. "That's like...That's gotta be, what, 15 inches, now? Maybe 20?"

Tanya wasn't interested in measuring the progression of the cold.

"I'm scared," she said. "Something weird is going on here, and I'd feel better if we just left."

"Oh, we're leaving, alright," said Kevin. He had already pulled his hiking boots out of the cubbyhole by the front door.

"We're leaving right now. I'm going to start the truck. You get Sadie bundled up. Don't worry about packing anything. I'll come back tomorrow to get our stuff."

Kevin was out the door then, his boots crunching on the snow that covered the driveway. It didn't surprise him in the least that the air outside the house felt warmer than the air that was creeping in from their cabin walls.

He unlocked the SUV, turned the key in the ignition, and breathed a small sigh of relief when the engine started easily. He had been afraid that he would come out to find his truck working no better than his stoves and his insulation.

Kevin took a minute to sweep a little snow off the vehicle, and then trudged back to the house.

"Let's go!" he shouted, as he walked back through the door. "The truck's ready to go!"

Tanya came rushing out of the bedroom, with Sadie in her arms, and a look of fear on her face.

"Kevin," she said, "the baby's burning up. She's got a fever—I just took her temperature, and it's high, *really* high. We have to get her to a hospital!"

And, suddenly, there was something more frightening than the mysterious things that were happening in the little log house.

"Okay, let's go," Kevin said. "Westlock's close."

And so, they left without bothering to lock the door or turn out the lights. They climbed into the truck and pulled out of the driveway, and Kevin drove as fast as he could all the way to town. Because the night was clear and calm, and the roads were bare and dry, they made it in record time.

Because it was Christmas Eve, the emergency room was quiet, and every member of the medical staff on duty was able to focus completely upon Sadie.

Tanya and Kevin stood off to one side, watching with growing alarm as the doctor and nurses dealt with their baby. Her fleecy sleepers were stripped off first, and her diaper followed. One nurse wiped her tiny body with a cotton pad that had been soaked in alcohol, while another prepared an ice bath. A third stood near Tanya and Kevin, saying calming things and coaxing information about Sadie's medical history out of them.

"Try not to worry too much," the nurse said. "I'm sure she'll be fine."

And, as it turned out, she was.

Four hours later, the doctor came into the room where Tanya and Kevin were sitting.

"Sadie's in good shape," he said. "That was a bad fever, but it's come right down. We'll keep her here for a day or two, to check for signs of infection, but I think she just caught a virus."

"Thank God," breathed Tanya.

"Ditto," said Kevin. He wanted to stand up and shake the doctor's hand, but he didn't trust the degree of strength in his knees.

Before the doctor walked out of the room, he turned and said one more thing.

"I don't want to frighten you," he said, "but it *is* good that you brought her in when you did. Fevers are scary things with little babies. Any later might have been too late."

The couple sat in silence for a few minutes, trying not to think about what might have happened. Eventually, Kevin turned to Tanya.

"Listen," he said, "there's some change in the console of the truck. Do you want a cup of coffee or something?"

Tanya nodded.

Kevin walked down the quiet hospital corridor and found the doors through which they had entered hours earlier. He pushed them open and walked out into the parking lot to yet another waiting surprise.

The calm, quiet weather of Christmas Eve had given way to a blizzard. The vast, nearly empty parking lot was hidden under a thick blanket of fresh snow, and the SUV had become a shapeless white mound. A powerful wind stung Kevin's bare face, and he could see—and feel—that it was coming from the north.

"This storm was right behind us," he said to himself, and he shook his head in wonder. Kevin looked at the whiteout around him, and knew that if they had left any later, they may not have made it to town.

By the time the sun rose on Christmas morning, the blizzard had moved on. In its place, there was blue sky and a fairy-tale landscape that was frosted with virgin snow.

Best of all, Sadie woke as sunny as the morning. She was hungry and alert, and too young to complain about spending Christmas in the hospital. When Kevin looked at her, he was no longer afraid and decided that it would be fine if he left for a couple of hours.

"I really should go and shut down the cabin," he told Tanya, and she agreed. After they shared some cold, soggy hospital toast, he was on his way.

Even with the four-wheel drive, the trip was dicey. Kevin took his time, particularly after he turned off the highway and onto the long, curving gravel road that would take him through Perryvale and on to the acreage. He knew that in the middle of the night, in the middle of the storm, with no visibility, driving would have been extremely difficult.

"*Might've* made it," he mused. "Sure wouldn't have made it as *fast.*"

When Kevin finally got to the cabin, he had to drive the truck back and forth several times, just to pack down the driveway and ensure that he wouldn't get stuck on the way out. When he got out of the truck, he grabbed a small shovel from the back, and used it to clear the formidable drift that had piled up against the cabin's front door.

When the snow had all been scooped away, Kevin leaned the shovel against the outside of the house. He took a deep breath and opened the door. He had no idea what he would find inside.

He found utter normalcy.

The cabin seemed snug again and cozy, although the fires had both died out hours earlier. Kevin held his hand against the wall and found that the air there felt no cooler than did the air in the middle of the room. He ran his hand along all the walls then, and around all the window frames, although it really wasn't necessary. He had sensed, as soon as he had walked in the door, that everything was alright. The cabin was welcoming once more. The cabin was warm. There were no ice crystals floating in the water that sat in the basin on top of the cast-iron stove.

"Well," Kevin said, out loud. "Huh." What he was thinking, but *not* saying, was much more incredible.

The house kicked us out of here, he thought. *Before it was too late for Sadie, the house made us leave.*

He was certain of it.

Kevin spent a good 20 minutes setting everything straight. He emptied the ash pans and took out the slop pails. He turned off the Christmas lights, which had been left to glow all through the stormy night. He locked the door at the back of the house and then prepared to leave by the front.

But before he closed the door behind him, he paused.

"Thanks," he said, to no one in particular. "See you next weekend."

By the time he reached the highway, he was missing the peaceful little cabin already, and he wondered, for the millionth time, why it was that he lived in the city.

Part 4

Angels

"Every time you hear a bell ring, it means that some angel's just got his wings."

—*It's a Wonderful Life* (1946), directed by

Frank Capra

Fourth and Willington

It was a good bench. Maybe even the best.

Roger felt well qualified to make such a judgment, because he had been sitting on benches, watching the world go by, for more than a year. Since his wife had moved away and he had stopped going to work, there was little else to do. So a good bench—a *really* good bench— was an important discovery.

He had tried parking his bottom in several different spots, all in the restful, green park he had nearly come to think of as his home. It was far enough from the gritty, wailing noise of downtown to be peaceful, yet close enough to the pedestrian action to be interesting. And it was full of benches—low stone benches in the middle of grassy expanses, wood and wrought iron benches beneath trees that gave generous shade, and even one marble bench, near the little drinking fountain. They were all nice; they all had their qualities. But the best of them was the rather plain two-seater, built of broad, smooth boards, at the corner of Fourth Street and Willington Avenue.

It was comfortable. It was seldom used by anyone else. And, while it sat within the hushed tranquility of the park, it offered a fine view of the world, as it existed at that inter-section.

Roger liked to watch the cars, the people and the little dramas that unfolded there daily. It was a fine, distracting form of amusement that kept him from focusing too harshly upon his own life and the fact that he had some-how allowed it to slip away.

Summer was the best. In the summertime, people bought their kids ice cream cones at the convenience store down the block, and then they would come walking past the park, as the heat caused rivers of melted strawberry swirl to run down their hands.

Spring and fall were nice, too. It was good to watch the trees become tinged with green and then burst into fresh foliage, and it was equally lovely to see those leaves turn golden and drift to the ground when their seasonal duty was done. The people changed with those seasons, as well. In the spring, they seemed more energetic, but still were less apt to rush. Come autumn, they appeared to be filled with purpose, prepared to buckle down to months of work after a summer of play.

It was only winter that could be drab. Snow piled up on the bench, and the people who walked past were in the business of keeping warm rather than providing entertainment. The skies were often gray, and the buses choked out clouds of exhaust that hung in the cold air and left it stinking. It was dreary, winter was, save for the few weeks leading up to Christmas.

The Christmas season was magical. In the last week of November, workers from the city would come out and wrap strands of tiny, white lights around the trees that grew in the middle of Fourth Street, dividing the two-way traffic, and around the gazebo that was the centerpiece of the small park across the way. Then they would move to the lamp posts that lined both the street and the avenue, and deck them with wreaths of feathery greenery and huge, red bows. The men and women who owned the little shops along Willington would string colored bulbs around their windows and under their awnings. And the people who traveled along those thoroughfares or patronized the shops or came to wait at the bus stop on Willington—those people all seemed happier than they did during the other winter months.

Roger would watch those people, filled with good cheer, burdened with shopping bags, and he would feel out of step. As much as he enjoyed watching the festivity, he knew that it no longer belonged to him.

Once, he overheard a woman talking to her husband as they stood at the corner waiting for the light to change.

"We have something for each of the children," she had said, "and your mother, and the Bensons. Still, we have at least six gifts left to buy, not counting each other."

Roger had been stunned. Had he ever done more than slip some cash into a card for his wife? He tried to remember, and found that he couldn't. It was another blurry area in a life that, over the previous months, had become increasingly indistinct.

There was something about all the decorations and happy shoppers that made Roger wonder how he had ended up where he was—on a bench watching other people live their lives instead of being busy with his own. There wasn't a single large mistake that he could recall, even on days when he was somewhat clear. There had been no desperately wrong turn, no one act that was fueled by pure stupidity or pure evil. He had done no great harm. Eventually, he came to realize that, because of a dozen socially acceptable character flaws—things like apathy and cynicism and procrastination—he had also done no great good. Understanding that had saddened Roger, but it hadn't changed him.

"People don't change," he told himself. "At least, not this late in the game."

And so, he sat in the park, and he thought about things, and he watched life pass him by. When it was necessary, he consoled himself with the knowledge that he at least had the vantage point of his really good bench.

Sometimes, what he watched from that bench was better than a movie.

Roger saw men and women arguing, sometimes quietly, through clenched teeth, and sometimes loudly, with broad gestures and colorful curse words. He saw kids skipping school to smoke cigarettes that they stole from the convenience store where their parents bought them ice cream. And he got to know all the regular people, people who walked past the bench on their way to work in the morning and on their way home at night.

Red Coat was one of those people.

That was the way Roger identified people, in his mind. He didn't know their names, so they became "Blonde Perm," "Down-filled Jacket," or "Yellow Book Bag." In less charitable moments, he had assigned names such as "Hook Nose," and "Missing Link." Generally, though, the names were simply for reference and not meant to be mean or even particularly meaningful.

Red Coat was a young woman—not much past a girl, really—who got off the Number Eight bus early each morning. From the bus stop on Willington Avenue, she would walk north along Fourth Street until she reached the building in which she worked. In the late afternoon, the routine was reversed—she would walk south on

Fourth Street and then cross Willington Avenue to board the same bus as it traveled in the opposite direction. Roger had noticed her but not paid her much attention, until she got the coat.

Before then, the girl had worn something that was not drab exactly, but ordinary. She had blended in with the rest of the commuters, in their overcoats of black and tan and olive green. But that November, in the same week that the city workers put up the lights and the wreaths and the bows, she had begun to wear the red coat.

It was obviously new. Roger could tell—from the perfection of the seams, the evenness of the nap and the way the hem still hung absolutely straight. But he could have determined it from the girl's expression alone. She looked proud when she wore that coat, and Roger imagined that she had saved her money for a long time in order to buy it.

There was something about that combination—the bright color of the garment and the obvious pleasure that the girl experienced when she had it wrapped around her—that Roger found enchanting. He found that he looked forward to seeing the girl each day.

Every morning, he would wait for Red Coat to emerge from the bus, looking like a vivid bloom against the dull foliage of the other commuters. It would make him smile to see her bright eyes and jaunty step, and the way she swung her hips beneath that scarlet wool, when she walked.

It's such a small thing, really, he would always think, *yet it has made such a big difference.*

Sometimes that made Roger wonder whether he shouldn't try to make some small, positive effort himself. It was a good thought, and he knew it, but it wasn't quite enough to pry him from his seat. He forgave himself for his lack of action, conceding that it was difficult to give up possession of such a truly first-rate bench.

The chilly December days marched on, and throngs of shoppers invaded the little stores along Willington, and the decorations looked lovely, and every so often, a group of carolers would take up residence in the gazebo. It all passed by with the same vague quality which Roger had come to expect of his days. The only vivid element woven through it all, the only *specific* thing that he could ever recall, was the happy girl in her crimson coat. She was the only person that caught his attention to the degree that he actually missed her when she was not there.

On Christmas Eve, she was not there when she should have been. On the morning of the 24th, Roger had seen her walking to work, carrying a bakery box which he presumed to be filled with some holiday treat for her co-workers. But long after the streetlights had come on, and the 5:15 bus had left the stop, and the sidewalks had almost emptied of human traffic, Roger had still not seen her head for home.

He realized that she may have caught a ride or taken a taxi, but it bothered him nonetheless. He remained, watchful, on the bench, long after he would normally have wandered off into the park. Eventually, his patience paid off.

Roger had been watching soft, white snowflakes drift down through the cones of space that were illuminated by the streetlights. He had heard distant footsteps and had looked up to see someone walking toward him from the far end of Fourth Street. It was Red Coat.

She was hurrying along the broad sidewalk, almost running, with her head bent over a creased sheet of paper. Roger imagined that it was a list of last-minute holiday preparations or directions to some festive Christmas Eve gathering. Whatever it was, she was intent upon it. Roger had been toying with the idea of speaking to her on this evening, of saying something friendly and normal, like "Merry Christmas." But the girl didn't look to be in a mood to speak with anyone.

With every step her boots scraped the concrete and sent up a little cloud of freshly fallen snow. When she got closer to Roger, he could hear the stiff swish of fabric as her coat brushed against her legs. He could hear her quick breath traveling in and out of her body. And he could hear a car engine in the distance.

Roger didn't usually pay attention to traffic sounds; he had grown accustomed to them as part of the natural atmosphere. But, for some reason, this vehicle—which he could not yet see—stood out as being significant.

As the girl in the red coat moved briskly toward the intersection, the car that Roger was somehow able to hear above all the others came into view. It was traveling west on Willington, *speeding* west on Willington more precisely, and Roger knew that the driver was planning to run the yellow light. Then the yellow light became a red light, and the girl in the red coat stepped off the curb, about to cross Willington to get to the Number Eight bus stop. She was still staring at the paper in her hand, oblivious to the car that was hurtling toward her.

Roger left the bench.

He left the bench with speed and strength that he had

not even been aware that he possessed, and he caught up to the girl. Before she was able to take one more step into the path of danger, Roger reached out and gripped her arm. He pulled her back with all his might, a split second before the car, its horn blaring indignantly, went speeding past.

The girl let out a startled, little cry. She gawked after the car, which had missed her by scant inches. And then she turned around to face her savior.

Roger hadn't done it for the glory. It had all happened so fast, he hadn't even had time to cultivate an *expectation* of glory. Still, he was disappointed by the girl's odd reaction.

When she turned to face him, she did not look grateful so much as she did confused. The expression of confusion rapidly changed into one of cold fear. Then, without expressing her thanks to Roger or even making eye contact with him, she turned and ran. Red Coat managed to make it across Willington before the lights changed again. The Number Eight bus pulled up then, and she disappeared into it.

Roger was left alone and dumbfounded.

Did I frighten her? he wondered. *Have I become one of those scary street people?*

But then, in one wonderfully clear moment, Roger realized that it didn't matter. It didn't matter what she thought of him; it didn't matter that there was no reward. She was safe, and he had saved her, and that was all that was important It was all the satisfaction he required.

Merry Christmas to me, he thought, and turned to wander back into the park, as it was his custom to do at the end of the day. He stopped when he saw someone standing beside his bench, looking at him.

It was a man in an impeccable dove-gray suit. His face was neither young nor old but shone with kindness. There was a sense of stillness about him, a sense of peace. When Roger met his gaze, the man smiled and held out his hand.

"Roger," he spoke, and his voice was deep and soothing. "It's time to go."

Roger hesitated—not out of fear, but out of confusion.

"I don't understand," he said to the man.

The man smiled, and made a small gesture in the direction of the intersection.

"You did great good, there," he said.

Roger shrugged modestly.

"I just grabbed her arm," he told the man.

"Sometimes," the man said, and he spoke very deliberately, "a small thing can make a big difference."

Roger noticed the bench then, with its thick, unbroken cushion of freshly fallen snow, and he knew that the kind man was right. It was time to go.

He nodded, accepting the invitation, and walked toward the man. He felt a protective arm drape around his shoulder. And he allowed himself to be led into the lovely, frost-trimmed stillness of the park.

Roger looked up as they entered. He saw the stone archway over the path, with its elaborately carved name. His mouth fell open.

"Have I been here all along?" he asked the man, as they disappeared into the deep blue shadows.

"All along," came the gentle reply.

From the minute she opened the door, she could tell that everyone was there and that the party had already started. There was laughter coming from the living room and the sounds of tinkling silver and glassware from the buffet that her mother would have already set up in the dining room. She was supposed to have helped to set out the food. She had been expected to arrange the gifts beneath the tree. She should have already changed into a fancier dress and curled her hair, but she was very, very late.

Not as late as I could have been. She made the grim joke to herself, as she hung her red coat carefully upon a wooden hanger in the front hall closet.

Her mother had heard the front door and came hurrying down the hallway. She was in her best silk dress, and the low heels of her new shoes clicked on the polished hardwood.

"Marlena!" she cried out, in an accent that imposed itself more heavily, whenever she was upset. "I was worried half to death! You never come home so late!"

"I know, Mama," Marlena soothed. "I'm very sorry. It's been a bad...well, a strange day. Did Peter help you with the food?"

"Never mind the food. Never mind Peter. What happened to you? You are looking very pale, I think."

Marlena saw the concern in her mother's face, and felt her own bravado crumble. Tears sprang to her eyes, and she handed her mother a worn, folded slip of paper.

"It's my notice," she said, and her voice quavered. "I lost

my job today. On Christmas Eve, yet. Nice, huh? This is what they call 'downsizing.'"

"Oh, that's so terrible!"

"I thought so, too," Marlena nodded. She had regained a measure of composure. "All afternoon, I was thinking *This is the end of the world*. But then, on the way home, Mama, I almost got hit by a car. It was so close." She held up her thumb and forefinger, nearly touching, to illustrate.

"I could have died, Mama," she said, "But someone grabbed my arm and pulled me out of the way."

"Oh, thanks to God!" Mama said, and crossed herself fervently.

"Yes," said Marlena. "Maybe more than you know. Because, when I turned around, Mama, there was no one there. No one at all, on the street. But, look."

She pulled up the sleeve of her blouse then, and showed her mother the place on her upper arm that was sore to the touch. It was red, all over, and bruises had begun to form there. Bruises in the distinct shape of fingerprints.

Mama looked at the marks, and looked at her daughter, and crossed herself, once again.

"I know," Marlena said. "It shook me up, believe me. But now, I'm just grateful. And now I feel like, 'What does a job matter?' There will be lots of other jobs. The important thing is that I am at home on Christmas Eve with you."

Mama wrapped her arms around Marlena then, and Marlena gratefully accepted the comfort of the embrace. It was several minutes before they pulled apart.

"Everybody is waiting," Mama said, and her voice was husky with emotion.

"Yes," Marlena nodded, and smoothed at the creases in her skirt. It was not what she had planned to wear, but what she wore really didn't matter.

Mama took Marlena's hand and led her down the hall, as though she was a little girl. Before they entered the rooms where the family was celebrating, she asked one question.

"Where did this happen? With the car, I mean?"

"Right on the street where I walk, every day," answered Marlena. "By the cemetery, there, at the corner of Fourth and Willington."

The Grocer's Gift

"I won't take charity."

"And I won't see you starve! Now take some groceries, Mattie. You've got to feed that baby that's inside you."

Mattie Denton lowered her eyes and a flush rose to her cheeks.

"So you can tell?" she asked the grocer, who stood on the other side of the worn wooden service counter.

The grocer's name was Ned Willis, and he had known Mattie from the time she was a girl. She had since become a full-grown, married woman but, considering the circumstances, Ned felt fully within his rights to meddle in her business. He looked into her pale face and shook his head with mock sternness.

"Of course I can *tell*, Mattie. You're thin as a bed rail, 'cept where it's starting to look like you swallowed a coconut."

Mattie felt embarrassed and hopeless, and she tried to lose herself in the folds of her thin, frayed coat.

Ned looked at the young woman closely and, suddenly, he understood another part of the problem.

"Jake doesn't know, does he, girl? You never told him."

"How could I tell him?" Mattie shrugged, and she looked at her friend with eyes that were circled by dark shadows. "You know Jake. He would have been beside himself, with worry. He had enough concern on his mind, just leaving me behind."

It was December of 1931. Jake Denton was Mattie's husband, one of many men who had been out of work since the onset of the Depression. That September, he had given up hope of ever finding employment in the little community the couple lived in, just northwest of Spokane.

"I'm gonna ride the rails south, Mattie," he had told his young wife. "I'll find work somewhere along the line and send money back to you."

Before he had left, Jake Denton did what he could to ensure that Mattie would be taken care of. He arranged a small line of credit at the local grocery store, with Ned Willis.

"I'll either be back here or I'll be able to send you some payment before that runs out," he had assured Ned.

But three months came and went, with no word from Jake. The leaves turned color, the snow began to fall, and Mattie Denton's line of credit was near its end. Being stubbornly independent, Mattie was more concerned about the situation than Ned Willis was.

"Alright, Ned. I'll take the biscuit flour and some tea, and maybe half a pound of sugar. But that's it. I won't be a burden to you."

Mattie stood as tall as she was able to and stuck out her chin. She didn't have much, but she had her pride.

"Oh for Pete's sake..." Ned rolled his eyes wearily and slammed a cardboard box down on the counter. He began to fill it with groceries, and as he moved around his store, pulling items from the shelves, he lectured Mattie Denton.

"Now, you listen to me," he said. "You folks always brought your business here, even when you could have saved a few pennies at the bigger stores, in the city. I always appreciated that. Now, I'm not going to stop supplying you your grub, just because you've fallen on a bit of a hard time. Also, I promised Jake he wouldn't have to worry about you going hungry, and I mean to keep that promise, no matter how bull-headed you intend to be, Mattie Denton. Now, have we got us an understanding?"

Ned Willis slid the box across the counter to Mattie. It was filled to the brim with groceries, and the very sight of them caused Mattie's mouth to water.

"But it's a handout," she complained.

"No," said Ned, and he shook his head decisively. "If you came in here askin', then I suppose, maybe. But I'm offering, and that makes it a gift, and it's plain *rude* to turn away a gift, especially at this time of year."

Mattie said nothing, but she was staring at the box, with its bounty of butter and eggs and fatty side-bacon.

Ned could see the hunger in her eyes, and he knew that he almost had her sold.

"Tell you what," he said. "Let's make it more officially gift-like, what do you say? I'll even include a card."

And with that, he grabbed a pen and a slip of paper, and scrawled out a few words. He reached across the counter and ceremoniously placed the note on top of the food.

Mattie looked at the note and smiled. It read *Merry Christmas from Ned.*

"This one time," she said, and she lifted up the box. Then she thanked Ned Willis for his generosity, walked out the door and took her marvelous gift home.

Home, for Mattie Denton, was little more than a two-room shack on the outskirts of town. Ned Willis's store was a good distance away, and the walk back to the house was made slower because of the heavy carton of food. Mattie didn't mind, however. It was a most welcome burden, and every time she stopped to rest, she would peek into the box and fantasize about the meal she would prepare herself that evening.

By the time Mattie walked through her front door, darkness was falling, and her hands and face were raw with the cold. She was exhausted but forced herself to start the little heating stove and set a pot of water upon it. While she waited for the water to boil, she took a potato out of the box of groceries and pared it with great care, making certain that no more than the tissue-thin peeling went for scrap. Then she cut it in four pieces and put it in the bubbling water to cook. When it was done, the potato went onto a plate, where Mattie mashed it with a fork, adding a small ration of the butter that Ned had given her. She pulled a small tin of corned beef out of the box, opened it with great reverence and put the meat on her plate next to the potato.

Mattie relished every bite. It was the best meal she had eaten in weeks.

I'm saved, she thought, with relief, as she collapsed into her sagging bed that night. *This will surely see me through until Jake gets back.*

But the weeks passed, and Jake didn't come back.

The winter grew harsher, and drifts of snow piled up around the little house. Freezing winds howled, night and day, and Mattie often stayed in bed for the warmth. Christmas Day came and went, with no celebration, and by New Year's Eve, the young woman was truly worried.

The larder was, once again, bare. Mattie was growing weaker with every day that her pregnancy advanced. The temperatures had plummeted, and the supply of heating fuel was nearly gone.

I won't make it; not without help, she finally admitted to herself, as she sat shivering next to the stove. Mattie knew that the kindly grocer would gladly help her again, but she also knew that her pride had caused her to wait until it was too late. She was too weak from hunger to walk to the nearest neighbor's house, let alone all the way to Ned Willis's grocery store.

So this is it, then, she thought, and she poured the last ounces of fuel into the stove. Then, frail, and despondent, Mattie Denton took to her bed. She assumed that she would never rise from it again.

Midnight passed, and 1931 became 1932. Come morning, pale light began to filter through the thin curtains that hung over the tiny bedroom window. The long hours of the day passed, and Mattie remained under the covers. The stove had stopped putting out heat and, since she had no reason to move, Mattie was determined that death could claim her in the relative comfort of her own bed.

Late in the day, however, as darkness descended and a fierce blizzard began to wail around the tiny house, Mattie was awakened by an unfamiliar sound.

Someone, it seemed, was knocking at the door.

I'm hallucinating, thought Mattie, and she wrapped the blankets more tightly around her thin shoulders. But the knocking persisted and, eventually, Mattie dragged herself out of bed and shuffled to the door.

"Who is it?" she whispered, though she pulled the creaky door open without much hope of finding anyone. Sure enough, she was met by only a blast of icy wind. Mattie cursed herself for being a fool and was about to push the door closed again when she saw that something had been left for her on the snow-covered boards of the front stoop. Three good-sized cartons of groceries sat next to two of the five-gallon pails that Ned Willis sold his heating fuel in.

"Oh, my Lord!" Mattie exclaimed. She knew that she was looking at her salvation.

It occurred to her then to look for her savior, and she peered out into the darkness, searching for the kind person who had delivered all of the goods. In the distance, past the gate to the road, Mattie saw a tall figure walking away, bent against the storm.

"Oh, thank you, Ned!" she said and raised her hand. Though the man could not possibly have heard her, he must have seen, for he raised his own hand in return. Then he vanished into the blowing snow, leaving Mattie Denton alone to enjoy her windfall.

It had been three full days since Mattie had eaten, and her last meal had been the stale crumbs of bread that she had found in the high cupboard, safe from the mice that ate everything within their reach. The very sight of food awakened a huge, gnawing hunger within her.

With sheer determination, she dragged in the loaded boxes and the two cans of what was indeed heating fuel. Mattie started the heater and grew nearly giddy when she felt a comforting warmth creep into the room. She went through the cartons of groceries and pulled out several eggs,

a stick of butter and a can of baked beans. Summoning her last ounce of strength, Mattie prepared a meal and allowed herself to gorge. Afterward, she returned to her bed, where she slept comfortably until the next morning.

She was certain that her supplies would last until Jake returned. Absolutely *certain*. And so, for more than a fortnight, she ate greedily and often. In the mornings, there were feasts of eggs and bacon or steaming bowls of oatmeal, heaped with melting sugar. At noontime, she often fried bread in a cast-iron pan on the stove and then smeared it with preserves. And, in the evening, there would be tinned meat or barley soup or a big bowl of potatoes or turnips, mashed with plenty of butter and salt and pepper. Mattie drank every cup of tea sweetly laced with honey and kept the house cozily warm and felt more satisfied, and well, than she had in months.

Mattie was growing stronger, but as January drew to a close, she was also growing concerned. There was no sign of Jake, no sign of a break in the severe winter weather, and her supply of groceries and fuel was once again dangerously low.

"Why didn't I ration it?" she asked herself, one day, as she took inventory. "Why didn't I make it last?" As she measured the fuel and counted out the few remaining tins, potatoes and ounces of sugar and flour, she began to feel desperate. For although her health had improved, Mattie was very pregnant. In her condition, with no proper winter clothing, she couldn't hope to strike out seeking help. She found it difficult enough to move back and forth between the two rooms of her little house.

"I'll just have to be very careful," she told herself. She began limiting herself to a few bites of food, each day, and wrapped herself in blankets, to stay warm, so that she wouldn't have to use much fuel.

For several days, she went on that way. She was strict with herself but, still, the supplies ran out. Once again, Mattie Denton took to her bed, knowing that she was destined to either freeze or starve.

And, once again, there came an unexpected knock on the door.

"Oh, Lord," she said, "please let it be either Jake or Ned Willis!"

Mattie dragged herself to the door and yanked at the frozen handle with all her might. Finally, the door opened with a loud groan, and Mattie saw that her prayer had been answered.

Another three boxes packed with groceries, and another two cans brimming with heating fuel, had been left upon her doorstep. Far along the road, beyond her own yard, the shadowy figure of a man was walking away.

"Oh, bless you, Ned," Mattie whispered. As if on cue, the man raised a friendly hand and went along his way.

Weak though she was, Mattie managed to prepare a huge meal. She ate ravenously and felt guilty afterward.

Here I am, preparing to make the same mistake all over again, she thought. Then she went to bed, promising herself that in the morning, she would take a careful inventory of her food and make a plan to portion it out over as long a time as possible.

After all, there was no telling when Ned Willis would be back, and Mattie was beginning to lose all hope of Jake ever returning.

In the middle of that night, Mattie was wakened by a pain that tore from her stomach straight through to her backbone. When it subsided, after several agonizing seconds, she berated herself for her gluttony.

I eat nothing for days, and then I eat enough for three grown men, she scolded herself. *I might have expected a bout of indigestion.*

But then there came another pain, and another, and another after that. And in the middle of the cold, lonely, little, two-room house, Mattie Denton miscarried the baby that would have been a son for her and Jake.

For several days thereafter, Mattie slipped in and out of consciousness. She lay in her bed, feverish and moaning. There was no one to care for her, no one even who knew of her misfortune. Finally, her fever broke, and Mattie grew lucid enough to understand that she alone would determine whether she was to live or to die.

She very nearly had to crawl, but Mattie left the bed and made it into the kitchen. There, she added fuel to the heater and opened a tin of fruit. After she had eaten, she felt a little better. It gave her hope that she might be able to carry on.

February turned to March, and the unmerciful blizzards finally gave way to warm, gentle breezes. Mattie Denton ate the good food that she had been given, and gradually, her strength returned to her. One day, she found that she could walk all the way to her front gate and back. The week after that, she could manage a short stroll along the road. Eventually, she felt well enough for a longer excursion, and she put on her Sunday dress, thinking that she would visit Ned Willis at his grocery store and thank him for his generosity.

Mattie had just stepped out of the house and closed the door behind her when she was startled by the appearance of a rough-looking man coming through the gate. He was unshaven and so thin that his clothes fairly hung from his bones. Mattie had been about to run back inside and lock the door behind her when the man looked up at her and smiled.

Mattie nearly fainted when she saw that smile. It was Jake, home at last.

"Mattie," he said, and they fell into one another's arms, and the long winter finally ended.

Two hours later, they sat together at the kitchen table. Jake was wolfing down biscuits and pan gravy with one hand. With the other, he still clung to Mattie, seemingly fearful of ever again letting her go.

"Ned Willis is a good man," he kept saying, between mouthfuls. "I thank God he was here to take care of you, because I rode those rails all the way to California and back, and couldn't find a day's worth of work. I ended up eating anything—garbage, seeds, anything. And the whole time, I was scared to death you'd be doing the same because you were too proud to go to Ned for help."

Mattie patted her husband's bony hand.

"I was too proud, at first," she said. "And then, by the time my pride was gone, so was my strength." Mattie told him about the baby, then, and how Ned Willis's timely deliveries had literally kept her alive. When she finished, there were tears in Jake's eyes.

"I'm so sorry, Mattie," he said. "I'm so sorry you had to

go through that alone, and I promise you that you will never have to go through anything alone, ever again.

"Now, as for Ned Willis," Jake continued, and he pushed his chair away from the table, "I think that he has waited plenty long to hear a 'thank you' from both of us. Let's walk over to the store together, Mattie. Today."

They set out together then, Mattie, in her Sunday dress and Jake, still looking like a scarecrow but in a clean set of clothing. They walked to the store, hand in hand, as enchanted with one another as they had ever been during their courtship.

The couple's blissful state was interrupted when they reached the grocery store. They found that the windows had been papered over, and the door, with its cheery bell, was solidly locked.

"Would he have gone out of business?" Mattie asked Jake. "After all these years?"

Jake stared at the blank-looking front of the deserted store and shook his head. Finally, he and Mattie asked an elderly passerby.

"Oh, my, haven't you heard?" the old man said. "We got to go all the way to the A & P in Spokane for our groceries now. Ned Willis passed away, here, just after Christmas, it was. His widda shut down the shop. It ain't been open since the New Year."

"Oh my God," said Mattie, and she gripped Jake's sleeve to steady herself.

"Thank you," Jake said to the old man as he wrapped a protective arm around his wife.

The couple turned around and walked home. They shared not a single word along the way.

When they got back to the house, they finally spoke of their sorrow over Ned Willis's passing. It was late into the evening, though, before Jake mentioned the mystery of the deliveries.

They were sitting at the kitchen table, drinking cups of tea and sharing stories of things that had happened over the course of the winter. At one point, there were a few moments of silence. Jake stared into his cup and then looked up at Mattie.

"I've been thinking—if you never got a good look at the delivery fellow—it must've just been someone else. That's the logical explanation, Mattie."

Mattie smiled at Jake, but shook her head.

"No," she said. "It was Ned. I know it for a fact."

"That's impossible."

Mattie stood up then and walked across the kitchen to the cupboard, where she had always kept her supply of groceries. She had kept something else there, too, and she reached up to the highest shelf and took it down. It was a small jam jar, and it held three rolled-up slips of paper.

"This was my way of keeping track," Mattie explained. "I wanted to make note of everything that Ned Willis gave me, so that eventually I could pay him back. So I wrote it all down, you see?"

She put the papers in front of her husband. They were carefully detailed lists, itemizing every last teaspoon of sugar and tin of sardines.

"This one, here—this is from the last time I was at Ned's store, back in December. But these other two, they're from the deliveries he made."

Jake looked at the lists and shook his head.

"I still don't understand," he said to Mattie.

"Well, this is the thing," Mattie said. "I had a pencil, but I didn't have any paper of my own. So I used his."

And Mattie turned the papers over, one by one.

On the back of each grocery list was a quickly scrawled note. The handwriting was identical on all three, as was the message.

Merry Christmas from Ned, each one read.

It was the unmistakable greeting of a kindly grocer, determined to keep his promise.

I am Your Brother

It was December 23, 1960. The man named Porter was hungry, tired and without a dime to his name. With the hope that there might be work for him in another city, he jumped aboard a freight train. The rocky ride jarred his aching bones, and the unbearable cold bit through his thin ragged clothing. He sank down into the corner of the box car in utter misery, resentful of those who were spending the holiday season with comfort and abundance.

Porter slept for a time, and then awoke to find that it was late afternoon and that he was in territory that was vaguely familiar. He stared at the distant mountains and the dense forest, and tried to remember when he had seen it before.

"There was a work camp here," he finally said to himself. The words had barely left his mouth in a plume of condensation when the camp that he had recalled appeared before his eyes. There was a clearing in the pines and a collection of tents around a larger makeshift shelter that Porter remembered as the cookhouse. Each of the dwellings glowed with warmth, and it was easy to imagine that a hearty meal was being prepared for the men.

They'll take me in, thought Porter. *There's food there, and shelter. Maybe even some work.*

And so, he looked for a soft drift of snow into which he could jump, and he let his body go limp, and in the practiced way of the hobo, Porter departed the train.

He had to follow the tracks back a way to get to the camp. As he walked through the frozen snow in his worn

shoes and tattered coat, he began to fear that he would not make it the whole way.

Sub-zero temperatures had turned his limbs into dull, thumping clubs. Starvation had turned his mind into a slow, useless thing. Exhaustion made the camp seem impossibly distant, even though Porter could see it from where he was. At some point, as he neared the tents with their inviting yellow lights, and tendrils of smoke curling steadily from their chimneys, Porter stumbled and fell. As it was much easier to close his eyes than to get up, that's what he chose to do. Porter drifted into welcome unconsciousness, where there was no cold, no fatigue, and he was mercifully unaware of the leaden emptiness of his belly.

He awoke in heaven.

Porter was sure of it, for he was on the soft mattress of a cot, with a feather pillow beneath his head and warm wool blankets piled on top of his body. But then he saw a black pot-bellied stove and a sloping canvas wall, and realized that someone had saved him by bringing him into the camp.

Porter turned his head a little and saw that at the foot of his cot a man stood watch over him. His face was lined, and his hair was bushy and gray. He wore work clothes that were patched and old, and his large hands were chapped raw from working in the cold. He said nothing to Porter, but Porter knew that the man was his savior.

"Thank you," he whispered. "What's your name?"

The man looked at Porter, and spoke in a voice that was soft and deep.

"I am your brother," was all he said.

Porter tried to sit up but was too weak. He wanted to ask the man what he had meant but felt too tired to pursue the matter. Ultimately, he closed his eyes and fell back into a warm, comfortable sleep.

Hours later, Porter awoke again, with his mouth and throat parched from the wood smoke. The very moment that he opened his eyes, the caring man was at his side, holding a dipper of cool water to his lips.

Porter drank until his thirst was relieved and then sank back onto the pillow. He looked gratefully up at his caretaker.

"Thank you, again," he said. "Who are you?"

"I am your brother," came the man's cryptic reply.

Porter simply nodded and closed his eyes. He was confident that there would be plenty of time to meet his benefactor, after he had slept just a little bit more.

The next time Porter awoke, he was amazed to find that he actually felt rested. He was eager to throw off the blankets, stretch his body and follow his nose to the source of the tantalizing, savory aroma which was wafting toward him from the opposite side of the tent.

Before Porter could even stand up, though, the man who had been caring for him was at his side. He handed Porter a tin plate heaped with eggs, bacon and thinly sliced potatoes fried in onions. There was bread, too— thick cuts of it, slathered with yellow butter, and a mug of strong coffee.

Porter nearly fainted at the sight and smell of such bounty. Without a word of thanks, he grabbed the plate from the man and began to wolf down huge mouthfuls of food. When every last crumb was devoured, and even the bacon grease had been licked from the plate, Porter looked at the man in shame.

"Thank you so much," he said. "I'm sorry to be so rude; it's just I haven't had a meal—a whole meal, like that—in I don't know how long. Still, I apologize. And I'd like to know your name, so I can say it more personal, if you know what I mean."

The man gazed at him, with his gentle eyes and his peaceful manner, and he spoke softly.

"I am your brother," was all he said.

"You know, I thought you might say that," said Porter.

There was nothing else to do then, and no one else around, so Porter put on his shoes and his coat and prepared to leave. He paused at the door of the shelter and spoke one more time to the man who had shown him such kindness.

"I don't know who you are, stranger, or how you knew I was out there, but you saved my life. I'll always remember that. If there was some way I could repay you, I would."

The man looked at him. Beneath his gray whiskers, there was a shadow of a smile.

"I am your brother," he said to Porter.

As Porter walked out into the cold, the thin light of dawn was beginning to crest the eastern horizon. He had spent an entire night at the camp and felt like a new man for having done so.

The work day starts early here, he thought to himself when he saw that there were no lights shining from the collection of tents which the workers bunked in. His next thought was of the town that he remembered to be no more than three or four miles up the tracks. With a well-rested, nourished body, he knew he could easily make the trek, and he set out without a single backward glance.

He arrived in the town that morning and found himself a few hours' work, and then met up with some fellows who lived much the way that he did. That evening was Christmas Eve, and they celebrated as they sat around a fire, sharing a bottle of liquor and some stories.

It wasn't long before Porter shared his dramatic story of the good Samaritan who had saved his life only the night before. The men listened to the tale, but looked confused and shook their heads.

"That can't be right," said one.

"You're either mixed-up, or lyin'," said another.

"What do you mean?" asked Porter.

The men looked at each other, and then one spoke.

"That work camp you're talkin' about; it ain't been up and runnin' for years. And that fella—that 'brother' fella—he sounds like Joe McTavish. But old Joe, he's dead and gone. Ages ago, he passed away. So, like Herman said, you either got things confused, or you're tellin' us one hell of a tall tale."

Porter didn't know what to say, so he said nothing, and spent the rest of the evening staring into the fire and doubting his own mind.

On Christmas Day, he had planned to move on. Instead, he found himself back-tracking, following the rail bed along the valley to the place where he was certain he had spent the night.

"I know that camp is here," he said to himself as he neared the spot. "It's right around that bend. I'll see it, and then I'll *know*, and then I can carry on my way."

But as Porter grew closer to the location, the odd feeling in his gut intensified. He could see no smoke curling up from the collection of chimneys he knew to be there; he could see no light shining from the cookhouse on the darkly overcast day.

When he turned the corner, he could see why. There was no camp on the site.

What was there, instead, were the snow-covered ruins of a camp that had once been. There were no standing tents, no people, and no friendly, warming fires. The only footprints in the snow were one lonely set leading from the large, weathered platform that Porter guessed might once have been the base of the cookhouse.

Porter looked at the tracks and set his foot into one of them. The fit was perfect. They were his own.

Disbelief and wonder and gratitude all swelled up within Porter at the same time. He stared at the bleak surroundings and shook his head. He would certainly have died there, beside the tracks, had it not been for the stranger who carried him to safety, kept him warm, allowed him to rest and filled his stomach with good food. The stranger had saved his life.

And then it occurred to Porter that he was not such a stranger anymore.

"Thank you, Joe," Porter said outloud.

A gust of wind blew through the tree tops, and in that whispering sound, Porter heard a voice.

"You are my brother," it said.

Porter moved on then. He walked back to the town and hopped another train and went on to other places and, eventually, to a better life.

Through the years, he did his best to be kind to others, particularly at Christmas time. It was his way of always remembering that he owed his very existence to a gentle spirit who taught him that no human being need ever suffer alone.

Personal Shopper

Albert Morgan was a desperate man. As such, he felt that desperate measures were in order.

"Look, you can take my credit card. Here's my bank card. And some cash! I have—let's see..." he said, and he began taking bills out of his wallet and throwing them on the desk in front of his secretary. "There's 40, 50, 55—$55, and you can keep that! Buy yourself something while you're out! A little something nice, huh?"

Donna, the secretary, looked up at Albert with a mixture of weariness and contempt.

"Look, Al," she said, as she pushed the pile of cards and cash back toward him, "don't get me wrong. It's not that I wouldn't *love* to do your Christmas shopping. It's just that I promised myself that I would no longer enable this sort of pathetic behavior in you."

"Not even for a hundred bucks?" he asked, hopefully.

Donna appeared to consider the offer but only for a second. She shook her head.

"No."

"Oh, come *on*, it's nearly Christmas Eve!" Al wailed in protest.

"All the more reason. I give you the gift of independence." Donna held her hands aloft, and stared dreamily into the distance as if she was reading a beautiful sign.

Al grabbed his money and his credit cards and stuffed them back into his wallet.

"Fine," he spat. "Just fine. But tomorrow morning, when Eileen opens her gift and *hates* it, because it's something *stupid*, because you made me shop for it all by *myself*, it'll be all your fault!"

Donna raised an unconcerned eyebrow and returned to her typing.

"Yeah," she said. "Why don't you try telling her that?"

Twenty minutes later, Al was navigating his car to the mall while he simultaneously tried to think of great gift ideas and plausible excuses for having selected the crappy gifts that he would undoubtedly end up buying.

"Why can't I do this?" he berated himself. "I run my own real estate office. I sell 100 houses a year. I buy the best suits, I golf with the mayor's brother-in-law, and I only weigh seven pounds more than I did in college. I'm successful. I'm pretty smart. And I only have to buy *one* lousy Christmas gift every year, just one! *Why do I always leave it 'til December 24th!*"

Al pounded the steering wheel for emphasis, and then pounded his own head in frustration. His breath was starting to come in shallow, little gasps, and he pulled frantically at the knot in his tie. The dash of the car appeared to tilt before his eyes.

"I don't believe this," he panted. Al recognized the onset of a genuine panic attack, something that the fates usually reserved for times when he had to speak at a sales conference or meet with his accountant. As his heartbeat quickened, the car slowed, and Al steered it clumsily into the shallow bank of snow that had been ploughed up against the side of the road.

And that's when he hit the old woman.

At first, he hadn't known. There had been a thump,

and the car had slipped a little on the ice. Al had been worried that he had bent a rim on some concrete parking curb that was concealed by the snowbank, and had gotten out of the car to investigate.

He had been cursing as he slammed the driver's side door, and continued to do so as he half-walked, half-slid, around to the front of the vehicle. The sight of the old woman there, sitting just inches in front of his grill, brought his stream of epithets to an end.

"Oh my God!" Al screeched. "Are you?...I didn't see you! Don't move! Let me grab my phone, and I'll call an ambulance!"

"There's no need, honey, but I would appreciate it if you would give me a hand up, and stop using all those sailor curses. Where you young people learn those terrible swears, I don't know. Could be the movies, I suppose. Hand?"

The woman held one gloved hand in the air. Al finally recovered from his shock, to a certain degree, and he took it. He eased the woman back on her feet, praying that when he got her there, both of her hips and legs would be in full working order.

They seemed to be. Al breathed a sigh of relief and began to apologize.

"I am so sorry," he said to the woman, as he dusted the snow from her dowdy, out-of-style, wool coat. "So, so, very, very sorry. I didn't see you there, and I was a little dizzy...Are you sure you're alright? Sure I shouldn't take you to the hospital or to see your doctor? How's your, uh, vision?" he asked, and waved a hand in front of the woman's face.

She flinched a little when Al nearly clipped her nose.

"It's fine, honey. *I'm* fine," she said. "You barely bumped me. Now, if you don't mind, I'll just be on my way."

The old woman tried to walk past Al, but he put an arm out to stop her.

"No, wait," he said. "I can't let you go. Not without, let's say, 50 dollars?" He pulled his wallet out of his suit jacket, and produced the money that he had collected from Donna's desk half an hour earlier.

The woman looked at him.

"Fifty bucks?" she said. "Is that the going rate for getting knocked on one's fanny?"

"You're right, you're right," Al said. "It's not enough." He paused then, nervously, before asking, "What *would* be enough?"

The woman shrugged.

"Well, heavens, I don't know. If I ran you down, what would you ask me for?"

Al looked stricken.

"I'd ask you to pick out a nice Christmas present for my wife," he said.

The old woman looked up at Al then, with a mixture of pity and understanding.

"Oh, my, you're one of those," she said. "My husband was one of those. My husband, Herbert."

"Herbert. Oh," nodded Al. He was once again enveloped in his own misery.

The woman looked Al over with a critical eye and seemed to come to a decision.

"My name's Olive," she finally said, "and I've decided that you can take me to the mall for a cup of tea."

The food court was crammed with last-minute holiday shoppers. Olive sat patiently at a tiny table for two, with her handbag resting in her lap. Al maneuvered through the throngs of people, carrying two Styrofoam cups. He made it all the way to the table without spilling and set the cups down with a sigh of relief.

"You know, it's sort of challenging to find tea here," he said. "I could have gotten you 15 different kinds of smoothies or one of those neon slush drinks. Did you know that you can buy french fries in a cup now? They pour this sort of gravy stuff all over them. You could nearly drink them with a straw by the time they're done."

"Thank you, I like my tea. Just black tea," she said, waving away the little packages of sugar and the plastic creamers that Al produced from his pocket.

Olive motioned for Al to sit. He did, but on the edge of his seat, with one knee jiggling nervously.

"Now, tell me about your problem, honey," she said, after she had taken a tiny, little sip of her tea.

Al heaved a sigh.

"I'm a last-minute shopper," he confessed. "And I never, *ever* manage to get Eileen anything good. Last year, it was socks. The year before was really bad—I got her a, uh, leg waxing kit from the 24-hour drugstore. It was the only place open. Other years, it's been brake pads, stationery supplies from the office, a bouquet of beef jerky samples..."

Olive held up her hand.

"Alright, I understand your problem," she said. "You may spare me the rest of the painful details."

"I tried giving her cash," Al continued, "but that never worked either."

"Oh, my!" Olive winced. "Honey, that's the worst!"

"But I'm lost, here!" Al cried. "And the stores are closing in, what, *90 minutes*, and that means that I'm as good as divorced in two hours. Because, I think this year is my last chance. I really do. We had a 'discussion' about this last month. And, you know, I promised her." Al pulled desperately at the collar of his shirt. His breath was getting a bit short.

"Well," said Olive, calmly, and she smoothed back a few strands of steel-gray hair, "a promise is a promise. You tell me a bit about your Eileen, and then we'll go shopping. We'll go together. I'll help you."

"Help me? You will?" said Al. The offer was unexpected, and the relief it brought was nearly overwhelming.

"Yes, I'll help you," nodded Olive. "Now, I want to know what she likes to do, and what her interests are, and where she's from. Tell me everything about her."

Al told her. Olive listened and made suggestions and sipped her tea. Fifteen minutes later, they were ready to take action.

"We're going to start with the Irish import store, over there,"Olive said. "You can buy her something nice, and—now this is important, honey, you might want to write this down—tell her that it reminded you of her pretty Irish name."

"Oh!" said Al, and he looked at his new friend with honest admiration. "Hey, that is good! That is really, really, good." He pulled out a notepad and pen, and followed Olive down the mall, scribbling down the wise things that she was saying. For the first time that day, he began to feel truly hopeful.

And, as it turned out, his hope was justified.

Before the stores closed, Al and Olive were back in the car, with several thoughtful, tastefully wrapped gifts. It made him feel nearly giddy to place the lovely packages on the back seat of the car. He was certain that Eileen would be pleased.

There was a feather-soft shawl from the import store, in complementary, muted shades of green and amber. There was a luxury bath set from another boutique, containing candles, scented oil and two impossibly thick, cotton towels. ("Tell her you hope to share that gift with her," instructed Olive, and Al had dutifully noted it down.) There were three antique silver picture frames, so that Eileen could display a few more of the old black-and-white photos she loved to collect, and a proper storage box for the rest of them, covered in a print of pink and red roses. ("The roses are a hunch," Olive had admitted. "I always loved pink roses, especially—and I think all women do.") Finally, there was the shimmering satin robe and dainty matching slippers, both in a beautiful shade of mist gray. ("Mauve would be my choice," Olive had said. "I've always been partial to mauve. But you say she's a redhead, your Eileen—so I think either the green or the gray.")

"I'm saved," Al said as he and Olive buckled their seatbelts. "You have *saved* me. You have no idea how grateful I am."

"Happy to help, honey." Olive smiled. "I wish someone would have given my Herbert a little direction, in the gift-buying department. He gave me a tape measure once for my birthday. He got it free, from the hardware store, with a five-pound bag of nails."

Al couldn't appear condemning. He knew he had done worse.

"But you stuck with him." he said to Olive.

She nodded.

"I always knew he meant well," she said. "I'll give a person a whole lot of leeway, when I know that they mean well."

"Well," said Al, and he pulled out his wallet and opened it, "I'd just like to thank you in a more tangible way. Here. This is for you." He held out two 50-dollar bills.

Olive eyed them, suspiciously.

"I see I've gone up in price since this afternoon," she said.

"No, really. You earned it. Take it, and buy something for Herbert or something for yourself," Al coaxed.

Olive shook her head.

"Honey," she said, "Herbert's dead. He doesn't need a thing. I don't need a thing, either."

But Al would not be rebuffed. He folded the bills in half, then reached over and opened the catch on Olive's black handbag. He dropped the money in, closed the bag and held up his hand to stop any protest.

"That's that," he said. "End of discussion. Now, where is it you live?" Al started the car and looked expectantly at Olive.

She was looking displeased and did not answer for several seconds. Finally, she waved her hand at him in a dismissive gesture.

"Oh, you might as well just drive back up Sixth Street. Back by where you ran into me," she said.

Al nodded and put the car in gear.

The drive was quiet. The conversation between Olive and Al had been coming very easily, but suddenly, conspicuously, it was not. Olive stared out the window at the Christmas lights that had begun to come on in the twilight, and Al cast nervous glances at his passenger, wondering how it was that he had managed to offend her.

"You know, I'm very grateful," he said, trying to draw her out.

Olive simply nodded.

"Never could've done this on my own," he added.

Olive gave no response.

Al gave up then. He decided that women in general could not be pleased and that he could never hope to understand them.

"Okay," he said. "I'll just drive. You tell me when to turn or whatever."

After several minutes of silence, Olive spoke, but not to offer directions. It was to offer advice.

"You have to remember, honey, a gift doesn't mean a thing if you don't put some thought into it. You could buy someone a luxury car, and it would be a shallow gesture if they didn't drive. But a little bag of their favorite penny candy—now *that* shows that you care about them."

Al nodded, trying to absorb the concept.

"I should write that down," he said. "I *will* write that down, when I get home, or when we stop to drop you off. Say, this is about where we, uh, *met*. Do I have to turn, soon? Should I get into the other lane?"

When Olive did not answer, Al glanced over toward the passenger seat.

There was no one in it.

"Holy! Oh my God!" Al yelled. He yanked on the steering wheel and brought the car to an abrupt and crooked stop at the side of the road. The vehicle that had been following him sailed past, its horn screaming and its driver making gestures that were out of keeping with the spirit of the season.

Al did not notice.

"Olive!" he shouted, as he made a frantic search of the car. There was no one in the back seat with the gifts. There was no one in the front seat with him. The passenger-side seatbelt was still buckled. And there was no way she could have opened the door and jumped out, not without him noticing.

"I've lost my mind," Al muttered. "This is the great, big breakdown I've been waiting for. It's finally here."

He felt lightheaded and short of breath, and the car seemed to be tilting back and forth.

"Not again," Al gasped. He pulled at his collar, put his head down and leaned on the passenger seat, for support.

His hand felt something other than upholstery there. Something papery and crisp. When Al felt somewhat calm again, he opened his eyes and looked over to see what it was.

It was the money—the two fifties that he had folded in half and dropped into Olive's handbag not more than 10 minutes earlier.

A gift doesn't mean a thing if you don't put some thought into it.

Al needed some fresh air. He stepped out of the car and closed the door behind him. As he breathed deeply, letting the crisp evening air clear his head, he noticed where he was.

He was across the street from the exact place where he had knocked Olive down.

And the exact place where he had knocked Olive down was in front of the tall, wrought-iron gates of a rather large cemetery.

It was then that Al wondered if he hadn't delivered Olive home, after all.

That Christmas morning was the best that Al and Eileen Morgan had ever shared.

"I love everything. I love *you*," Eileen said to Al, and the way her eyes shone as she said it made Al want to go shopping for her all over again.

Of course, he didn't say that. He said something jokey instead, something about the gifts just being a few little trinkets that he had picked up on his travels.

"Well, they're great," Eileen assured him. Then she looked him in the eye, and put on an expression that told him that she didn't want a funny line for an answer, and said, "But you know that it's not the stuff, or what it cost, right? Do you understand that I'm happy because of the *thought* you put into this?"

Al nodded.

"I think I finally do understand," he said.

No one really wanted to buy or sell a house in the week between Christmas and the New Year. Al opened the office for a couple of days, but it was a casual couple of days, a chance for everybody to catch up on their paperwork.

Donna was at her typewriter, wearing blue jeans, a sweatshirt and a ponytail. Al walked past in his jogging suit and rapped his knuckles lightly on her desk.

"Goin' out," he said. "I'll be back in a couple of hours."

"I'll try not to wither from loneliness," Donna mumbled, without taking her eyes off her work.

Al paused at the door as he put on his coat.

"Can I get you anything while I'm out?" he asked.

Donna stopped typing and gawked at Al.

"Get something? For *me?*" she asked, in disbelief.

"Yeah," said Al. "A muffin? Or a sandwich? Maybe one of those things you like—those, those, what do you call it—mocha-coffee things?"

Donna stared at Al, too stunned to answer.

"That's okay, never mind," Al said. "I'll surprise you."

He walked out the door then, and left Donna gaping after him.

"*Surprise* me," she said, to herself. "You couldn't possibly surprise me more than you just *did.*"

Al stopped at the florist's first, where he picked up a special order and paid for it with the two folded 50-dollar bills that he had been saving in the secret compartment of his wallet. Then he got back into his car and drove down Sixth Street until he reached the gates of the cemetery where he had met Olive on Christmas Eve.

He didn't know her last name, and he was operating largely upon a hunch, so he expected that his search would take a while. In the end, he spent just over an hour trudging through the snow, reading grave markers, before he found the one that he was looking for.

"Olive Peterson," it read, "Beloved Wife of Herbert." Al noted that "Herbert, Beloved Husband of Olive," was parked right next door.

Al cleared his throat and took a quick look around to ensure that no one was within earshot.

"Hi, Olive," he said. "You, ah, gave me a little scare back there in the car, but I guess I know why you had to make such a quick exit. Didn't want to miss your stop, huh? Don't blame you. It's a nice place you've got here. Quiet neighbors, and all...Anyhoo..."

Al harrumphed again, nervously. He took a moment to gain his composure and then continued in a more serious tone.

"Eileen really liked the presents," he said. "And I wanted to thank you again. Properly, you know, and I've been thinking a lot about what you told me. So I got you something. A little something..."

He stepped forward then and set the florist's arrangement on top of Olive's grave.

"It won't last long, because it's so cold, but I thought you might like it, anyway. Pink roses. They're your favorite, right? And, uh, the ribbon, there. I told them 'It has to be mauve, because mauve is the color that Olive likes best!'"

Al laughed a little bit and then grew silent. He felt the peace of the cemetery settle around him like a soft down comforter.

"You see," he said, quietly, "I get it, now. Thank you for showing me."

Al kissed his hand, and held it up toward Olive's gravestone in a simple gesture of farewell. Then he turned and walked back through the snow to his waiting car.

The floral arrangement was a spray of vibrant color atop the blanket of pure snow that covered Olive's grave. The roses were blush pink and perfect and tied together with just the right amount of baby's breath and feathery greens. Starched loops of mauve ribbon fanned out behind the flowers, creating a fanciful backdrop, and then wound down around the stems. At the very bottom of the bouquet, the ribbon laced through a hole that had been punched in a small, square card.

On the front of the card, there was a picture of a pale, pink rosebud. Beneath the illustration, Al had written three short words.

It's the thought.

Al Morgan had finally learned which part of the gift it was that mattered.